SPECIAL EDUCATION SERIES
Peter Knoblock, Editor

Achieving The Complete School:
Strategies for Effective Mainstreaming
Douglas Biklen
*with Robert Bogdan, Diane L. Ferguson,
Stanford J. Searl, Jr., and Steven J. Taylor*

Classic Readings in Autism
Anne M. Donnellan, *Editor*

Stress in Childhood:
An Intervention Model for Teachers
and Other Professionals
Gaston E. Blom, Bruce D. Cheney,
and James E. Snoddy

STRESS IN CHILDHOOD

An Intervention Model for Teachers and Other Professionals

GASTON E. BLOM
Boston University School of Medicine

BRUCE D. CHENEY
Michigan State University

JAMES E. SNODDY
Michigan State University

TEACHERS COLLEGE PRESS

Teachers College, Columbia University
New York and London

Published by Teachers College Press, 1234 Amsterdam Avenue,
New York, N.Y. 10027

Library of Congress Cataloging in Publication Data

Blom, Gaston E.

  Stress in childhood.

  (Special education series)
  Bibliography: p.
  Includes index.
  1. Stress in children. 2. School children—Psychology.
3. Student adjustment. 4. Teacher participation in
personnel service. I. Cheney, Bruce D., 1931– .
II. Snoddy, James E., 1932– . III. Title.
IV. Series: Special education series (New York, N.Y.)
LB1117.B565 1985   372.18'019   85-14825

ISBN 0-8077-2780-6

Manufactured in the United States of America

91 90 89 88 87 86   1 2 3 4 5 6

Contents

Preface

Children are subject to stress-inducing environmental events and situations just as adults are. Parents and educators have been slow in recognizing this, at least to the extent required to develop the knowledge and skills necessary for effective interventions. Yet teachers are in an excellent position to help children learn how to deal with stress, by virtue of their prolonged daily association with them. This book provides a stress-intervention model that teachers and other caregivers can apply without becoming therapists, a role for which they are not often prepared. It also suggests time-efficient interventions adaptable to a teacher's role.

It is difficult to quantify the impact of stress on children's academic learning and school adjustment, but it is safe to say that for some children it is a major impediment to achievement and that most children occasionally are diverted by the effects of stress. Children's responses to stress vary widely. A few become seriously incapacitated, the majority adapt with defensive and coping behaviors, and a small group do very well in the face of adversity. These latter children are described in this book in order to acquaint the reader with their remarkable coping skills in responding to stressful events or chronically stressful situations. The importance of this group exceeds their small number in two respects: (1) they illustrate that stress can be a challenge rather than a threat; and (2) the possibility exists that the coping behaviors that these children have learned may be taught to other children.

Children experiencing stress, as well as their behavioral responses to it, are described in ample variety by means of vignettes scattered throughout the book. The stress-intervention model, placed as it is within a context of real examples, becomes the process guide for teachers to use in considering each child's situation before deciding whether, how, and to what extent to intervene. The model is practical in helping teachers recognize that effective interventions are sometimes simple and time efficient for busy professionals. It is also realistic because limitations to the model are recognized; it is not offered as foolproof.

Both reactive and proactive interventions are discussed and illustrated in the book, but the emphasis is on the reactive. With information and skill, the teacher's reactions to a child in stress will more likely be sensitive and appropriate. Even at rarer times when teacher intervention is inappropriate, it will not be harmful, as some teachers fear.

The tone of the book is practical and encouraging, suggesting that teachers can effectively help children experiencing stress most of the time by using their own skills directly or, when necessary, by referring the children to others who have specialized knowledge.

The teacher groups with whom the contents of this book have already been shared in practicum situations have responded enthusiastically to its purpose as well as to the stress-intervention model as a tool. Teachers in the pilot groups have had no difficulty identifying children in their classrooms who were experiencing stress. They have typically been reassured to find that others share their concern for children in stress and that practical suggestions are available that help teachers respond effectively.

Based upon our experiences with this material, this book should appeal to elementary teachers and special education teachers, both those currently teaching and those who are near the end of their undergraduate preparation programs. Consequently, the book should be usable in both graduate and undergraduate courses. Elementary principals and other professionals who work with children in the elementary school setting, such as counselors, school psychologists, school social workers, and school nurses, also have expressed interest in the information included. We believe that parents of children also will find this book informative and useful in their relationships with their children, even though it is not written specifically for parents' use.

In this regard, our book is a departure from the number of books about stress in childhood that have been written from the perspective of the psychoanalytic theory of personality development. They tend to emphasize the dangers of stress and possible psychopathological outcomes. The psychoanalytic theoretical model of stress is a complex one and does not readily suggest helpful interventions other than psychological support, sensitivity of adults, and measures based on special clinical training. Works based on the psychoanalytic model include a variety of stress events: death of a parent, rape, accidental injury, hospitalization, child handicap, divorce, remarriage, adoption, family moves, first days of school, and natural disasters. At times the concept of "stress" includes such a wide range of psychological states (anxiety, conflict, and childhood developmental events) that the term loses its specific definition and meaning. While our book will discuss some of these same states and events, our concept of stress will be limited to clearly identifiable acute or chronic life events or situations that impinge on the child's life.

In addition, there are a great many children's books with bibliotherapeutic intent that deal with specific stress events and situations of childhood. These include divorce, one-parent families, death of parent, hospitalization, a handicap, and others. The present volume includes references to a number of these books, together with suggestions for their use.

Although the literature in the area of stress in children in school is limited, the literature related to the larger areas of stress in children is growing, and of course the general field of stress contains both research and theoretical literature. Selected references are included from these areas as well.

The knowledge, theoretical models, research, and teacher procedures that are presented in this book are the result of four years of collaborative work by the three authors. The material has been used on numerous occasions with advanced undergraduate students and graduate students engaged in master's and doctoral study. They come from the fields of elementary classroom teaching, special education, reading instruction, school counseling, teacher education, counseling psychology, and measurement and evaluation. All the groups and classes that have used this material have been very receptive and enthusiastic.

STRESS IN CHILDHOOD

An Intervention Model for Teachers and Other Professionals

1

The Experience of
Stress in Children

• Jerry Meyers, a third grader in Mr. Sloan's class, seemed to get along pretty well in school. His schoolwork was about average, and he seemed well adjusted. He had three or four friends, all boys, with whom he associated most of the time, but he played with other children occasionally and he seemed well liked by his classmates. Around the middle of March, Jerry's behavior began to change slightly; he seemed less attentive to his schoolwork, and he quarreled more often with his friends. When Mr. Sloan first noticed these changes in Jerry's behavior, he wondered not only what might be causing the changes but also how long the new behaviors might continue. Since he did not notice any significant changes in the relationship between Jerry and himself, Mr. Sloan decided to create opportunities for the two of them to talk. If Jerry were having real problems, they might come out in one of these conversations. Mr. Sloan simply made times when they could be together in semiprivate situations. Jerry offered no leads in these discussions.

In a conversation with Ms. Holcomb, the school principal, Mr. Sloan found out that Jerry's mother had told Ms. Holcomb that, while the decision was still up in the air, the Meyers family had known since the last of February that Mr. Meyers was likely to be transferred to the East Coast over the summer and that the family would be moving before fall. Now Mr. Sloan had a clue to the changes in Jerry's behavior. Perhaps he was anxious about the likely family move and all that it entailed for him: a new home and new room, no friends, a different school, a new teacher whom he would not know, a strange neighborhood, moving far away from both sets of grandparents, and on and on. Remembering how he felt when his own family moved during his fourth-grade year, Mr. Sloan wondered what he could do to help Jerry. No one had recognized how upsetting the move had been for Mr. Sloan as a child. In his attempt to appraise the situation, Mr. Sloan's reasoning went this way: If Jerry had not revealed his concern about the possible move, perhaps he just didn't want to share his feelings with someone outside the family. Or perhaps Jerry was afraid Mr. Sloan would not understand his fears or consider him a sissy, or perhaps Jerry couldn't verbalize his fears because he didn't understand them. Yet it was possible that other family members were anxious about the move as well and might not be psychologically aware or available to offer Jerry much support at this time.

Mr. Sloan finally decided to honor Jerry's reasons for silence, particularly since he wasn't absolutely certain Jerry's behavior changes were caused by his anxiety over the move. Yet he wanted to do something for Jerry, particularly since Jerry had developed into a minor behavior problem in the classroom. As it happened, Mr. Sloan had already established regular biweekly class discussions on topics of interest to the children. Sometimes the class would select the topic, sometimes Mr. Sloan. So the topic of "Moving to a New Town or New School" was placed on the agenda.

Mr. Sloan knew there were five children in the class who had moved into the school neighborhood over the past summer or during the past school year. During the discussion, he drew these children into talking about how they had made new friends and about how they felt when they came to the new school for the first time. About one-third of the children told about moves their families had made since they had entered kindergarten over three years ago. Because Jerry did not enter into the discussion, Mr. Sloan believed his attempt to help him had failed; yet within a day or two Jerry seemed to be more interested in his school work, and he even seemed to get along better with his old friends. Mike and Jerry began to play together on a regular basis. Mike was one of the five children who had moved into the community during the past year.

Jerry seemed to get along reasonably well for the remainder of the school year. His family did move over the summer, and Mr. Sloan wondered how Jerry got along but never saw or heard from Jerry again, as is often the case for teachers.

The following fall, at the end of the second week of school, Angela was transferred into Mr. Sloan's third-grade class, one of seventeen children who were transferred to his school from other nearby schools, to adjust class sizes. Angela's school transfer did not involve a family move, but, remembering Jerry's responses to his family's move, Mr. Sloan was particularly observant of Angela for the first few days.

Fortunately, Angela, who had been an above-average student, continued to do good work and, with her outgoing personality, made friends very quickly. This was probably made easier because two children in Mr. Sloan's class lived almost directly across the street from Angela. After a few weeks Mr. Sloan decided that the transfer had had little negative effect on Angela, yet he realized his experiences with Jerry the preceding spring had caused him to be more sensitive to such events in the lives of his pupils.

Stress is a regular part of everyone's life, including children. In the lives of children the events and conditions that may be stressful may be different from those that are stressful for adults. Something in Jerry's life caused a change in his behavior at school, and it was probably his concern over the possible move. On the other hand, the move from one school to another caused Angela no apparent difficulty. She seemed to adjust to her new school situation in such a way that she did not change her behavior in school, as Jerry had.

The two cases—Jerry's and Angela's—are alike, and they are different. Both involved a significant life event; for one a family move, for the other a change of schools without a family move. In Jerry's case, his change in behavior was a signal to the teacher that he was experiencing stress, while with Angela an event that had the potential to be stressful apparently was not. Jerry's stress, however, may have been greater due to the greater change that a move to another community entails.

Definition of Stress

For teachers and other human service professionals, understanding stress in order to be helpful to clients, both adults and children, is fundamental. Operational definitions of stress and some related concepts are important. Stress involves two components: a stressor and the individual's response to that stressor.

A stressor is an acute life event or a chronic environmental situation that causes disequilibrium in the individual. This disequilibrium is sufficient to cause the person to make an adjustment to the stressor. This adjustment is called a response. When both a stressor and a response to it occur, stress is present.

Stressors are often thought of as life events and situations that are unpleasant; however, sometimes events and situations that are usually considered pleasant, happy, rewarding, or successful can be stressful. A person may respond to a stressor with either maladaptive or adaptive behaviors. Different types of stressors and possible responses are represented in the following examples, as they pertain to children:

1. A child hides in her bedroom when her parents quarrel—an unpleasant condition associated with maladaptive response.
2. A child who is in the hospital for surgery reacts with unusual optimism and courage—a potentially unpleasant event with an adaptive response.
3. A child who is placed in a prestigious program for gifted and talented children demonstrates a noticeable increased interest in his school work—a potentially rewarding event with an adaptive response.

The capacity of a child to respond adaptively to an event or a condition varies widely. The greater the number or severity of challenging or threatening events or situations, the more this capacity is tested.

It is important to consider events and situations as *potential* stressors. Almost every experienced teacher can assemble a long list of potential stressors, including events such as separation from one or both parents, losing a glove or overshoe, being "picked on" by peers, and a trip to the dentist. Also included are conditions such as a physical handicap, a parent with a chronic drinking problem, and severe poverty. These events occur and these situations exist regularly in the lives of many children. How each child responds and how teachers can assist children are the central themes of this book.

A Teacher's Retrospections on Childhood Stress

Sometimes it is helpful for a teacher to think back, to retrospect, on a stressful event or condition in his or her own childhood. One teacher who did so remembers the following incidents:

• When I looked back at my childhood and attempted to mark an incident that changed my behavior significantly, I remembered a series of events that did exactly that.

I used to wonder why I was so afraid of snakes. This fear was in such contrast to my early behavior and attitudes. When I was about four or five years old, I used to go into the fields around our house and catch snakes. I can remember having bottles lined up around our basement with a snake in each one. I remember the excitement and thrill of holding a baby snake and the fun we had when a snake got loose in the house and hid in the furniture.

Then there was a blank spot in my memory. For a few years I could not remember what happened next. I have a feeling that some other boys were in the field with me and that I was frightened but I couldn't remember any more. What I did remember was a little boy in our neighborhood coming home after being bitten by a snake. I remember him crying and screaming all the way down the street and blood all over his hand. It was terrifying. Later, I wondered if that little boy might have been me. Another memory was about boys in the neighborhood throwing snakes into the leaf fires and the strange smells of the snakes burning alive. I wonder now if that really happened. I can also remember nightmares about snakes all around my bed.

To make matters worse, my sisters discovered a wonderful way to torture me. One sister brought in a live snake and stuck it in my face when I wasn't expecting it. I reacted in such a hysterical fashion that both my sisters were encouraged to invent new tortures. They used to wrap the vacuum cleaner hose around their necks like a boa constrictor and then surprise me by calling for me to come help. When I would find them writhing on the floor with this thing around their necks, I would absolutely fall apart. They would erupt into gales of laughter and I would cry hysterically.

My fear increased to the point at which I could not be in the same room with a snake. I attempted to deal with this through compulsively reading everything I could about snakes, watching for them on television, and carefully approaching the subject without ever coming too close. I still had the nightmares and embarrassed myself a few times by becoming hysterical in front of others, but generally I was able to control and somewhat hide my fear of snakes.

Then I found out what had happened to cause my fear. My mother told me that when I was about eight years old, some older boys forced my hand down a garter snake hole. The garter snake actually bit me, and I was the little boy who came home screaming with the snake bite. I was very much relieved to understand finally what had caused my drastic change in attitude about snakes. However, I now have another question. Knowing something of the symbolic meaning of snakes, I wonder if something else might have occurred on that day that I cannot remember and my mother never knew about. With the past ten years or so my fear has been greatly reduced, but I have not yet gotten to the point of touching or holding a snake, even a small one, with ease.

During the ten years of my greatest fear, my mother was very supportive. I could run to her when I was afraid, and she could protect me because she was not afraid.

As I think back, I realize I was best able to control my fear when I had some control of a situation. If I was moving toward a snake, I was all right, but if someone else was moving toward me with a snake, I would panic and lose control. It was fortunate that my parents did not push the issue but recognized the intensity of my fear. At no time was I ever forced into a situation in which I would have to touch or hold a snake. My parents' support helped me feel a sense of control over most situations involving snakes.

Not every teacher's memories of childhood will be as dramatic and prolonged as those described. Yet what is portrayed in this example captures common childhood happenings such as being victimized by others and having one's vulnerabilities and fears exploited. There were both open fears known to other people and silent fears that were known only to the teacher as a child. Events happen that parents are not aware of and children keep hidden from them. Under those circumstances as a child grows up the contents of events are gradually suppressed from memory and become blank or distorted. Yet the feelings around these events retain an active influential power. At some cognitive level this teacher had an awareness of the symbolic meanings of snakes. He was able to recall his early childhood innocence at four or five years of age and the change at eight. The realistic fears of snakes and the complex events surrounding these fears became a central focus of concern throughout childhood, with repeated attempts made to master and conquer them. The preceding example is just one in a wide variety of recalled childhood events that a teacher can use to heighten awareness and sensitivity in working with schoolchildren.

Highlights of Studies on Stress in Children

The subject of stress in children has not received sufficient attention, particularly from the perspective that teachers and other school professionals can or should be knowledgeable about stress so that they can assist children in developing positive responses.

Early work on stress focused on the biological aspects of the immediate response to stress, with Cannon (1929) developing the notion of "flight or fight." These responses were characterized as the "wisdom of the body," that is, the body's inborn capacity to respond automatically to stressors.

Hans Selye (1956) investigated the psychobiological responses of people to physical stressors and developed the concept of the "general adaptation syndrome," or the progression of body responses to stress over a prolonged period of time.

Interest in the biological responses to stressors continues today, while interest in the psychological responses has also developed. These two areas of study have a number of parallels, yet the work on each also moves ahead independently. Much of the "stress management" efforts currently enjoying considerable popularity tend to focus on techniques individuals can employ to control the biological responses to stressors. It will be readily apparent to the reader that the interventions recommended in this book tend to deal with and attempt to control, alter, and/or maintain selected psychological responses to stressors. However, it is necessary to keep in mind that the biological dimension of response exists and should be acknowledged.

Holmes and Rahe (1967) were interested in various life events and the relationship of these events to the occurrence of disease. They developed an evaluation instrument, called the "Schedule of Recent Experience," which was a list of forty-three life events such as a minor law violation, a change in residence, getting married, being jailed, and death of a spouse. Each of the life events was assigned a weighted score, and the scores were totaled for a given individual. Holmes and Rahe found a weak but positive correlation between the life events total score and the onset of illness; that is, they found that the number and severity of the life events a person had recently experienced were marginal predictors of the likelihood of that person becoming ill in the near future.

Coddington (1972) conducted research developed partially from the work of Holmes and Rahe. He relied on teachers, pediatricians, and child mental health workers to develop his "Life Events Questionnaire," which included a different set of life events for preschool, elementary school, junior high school, and senior high school students.

By administering this questionnaire to a child or adolescent, the extent of social-psychological adjustment that a person had undergone during a specific time period could be determined and related to the onset of illness or emotional disorder.

Garmezy (1981) employed a somewhat similar method of measuring the number and significance of the stressors in a child's life, through a stress inventory. However, he was more interested in the nature and range of responses children make to stressors. Specific life event items were added to and deleted from Coddington's questionnaire; he then used the modified survey instrument as a rough quantitative measure of stress in a child's life. Those life situations that were found to have high chronic stress he termed "at-risk" situations, and he has devoted much of his research to those children he considers to be in those situations.

Holmes and Rahe, Coddington, and Garmezy all have used some form of stress inventory. These inventories include a limited number of life events, and they all suffer from the disadvantages of undetermined validity and inadequate reliability of their ratings. However, they are helpful for teachers in that they focus attention on the range of events and conditions in the lives of children.

Lazarus (1966, 1977) focused on acute medical and environmental events in the lives of adults. He attempted to make distinctions between defense mechanisms and coping modes. He also included, as a part of the response pattern, the person's cognitive appraisal of an event in determining the extent of the threat and the available resources for dealing with the threat.

There are some books and published reports on stress in children's lives. The most important of these include the works of Ann Kliman (1978), Gilbert Kliman (1968), Thomas Cottle (1980), Susan Ramos (1975), Martha Wolfenstein (1977), and Susan Wolff (1981). These books are written from the perspective of psychoanalytic developmental theory and tend to emphasize the dangers of stress and possible psychopathological outcomes. As we stated in the preface to this book, such a perspective has its limitations, and none of these books are specifically directed at a teacher audience.

Anthony (1974) has pointed to stress as creating vulnerability and consequent adverse reactions. However, along with Garmezy (1981) and others, Anthony has identified children who do extremely well under very adverse chronic conditions. These at-risk children have been tagged with the exaggerated labels of "invulnerables," "children who will not break," and even "superkids." Chapter 13 of this book is devoted to these remarkable children.

Those who have written about stress in children from the particular perspective of the school include Rutter (1979), Phillips (1978), and Olweus (1978). Rutter did an extensive study in the secondary schools of London, with a focus on those mediating variables within the school that modify students' adaptation patterns in both favorable and unfavorable ways. School bullies and their victims were investigated by Olweus, as were the roles and effectiveness of selected interventions in school settings. Phillips' work dealt with school-based anxiety and stress independent of out-of-school events and conditions. The stressful nature of schooling and its adaptive and maladaptive efforts were examined.

A number of specific stressors of childhood have been studied in depth. For example, Wallerstein and Kelly (1980a, b) did a longitudinal study of children of divorced parents in California. Helfer and Kempe (1968; Kempe and Helfer, 1980) have studied child abuse and neglect problems. Blom has been involved in and studied school-related disasters such as a tornado (Blom, 1980a) and the falling of a school street crosswalk during the time children were coming to school (Blom, 1981). Blom (1958) has also reported on the stress of childhood illness and hospitalization.

There are many books for children in the realistic fiction genre that deal with stress events and situations of childhood such as divorce, one-parent families, death of a close relative, hospitalization and others. Because of the potential of such stories for assisting children in responding to stressors, children's literature is discussed in chapter 15 of this book.

Needs Assessment Study with Teachers

Zucker and Snoddy (1980) surveyed both preservice and inservice teachers relative to their reported behaviors and attitudes toward stress in children. Forty-seven student teachers from three student teaching centers and thirty-six experienced teachers from four different communities responded to the survey. These teachers were provided with a list of common stressors for children and asked to indicate (1) whether or not they were aware of these stress events and conditions in the lives of the children they taught and (2) if so, how they as teachers responded to those children experiencing stress.

The study reveals that elementary teachers are well aware that children in their classrooms are involved in acute and chronic stress situations in school and at home. Teachers report that they are willing to listen to children and that children see them as potential sources of support. However, the teachers report that the educational system does not provide them with curriculum, materials, facts, or skills with which to implement beneficial interventions.

It appears that teachers are reporting a predicament. They know that many of the children in their classes are experiencing home problems, but they have little personal and professional preparation for helping. At times, someone outside the family is the only available resource for help, but teachers hesitate to venture into these areas as classroom topics.

While it is disheartening to find that teachers generally feel inadequately equipped to help children experiencing stress, it is encouraging to learn that many teachers would like to be better prepared to assist them. Recognizing that teachers are not trained as therapists, one might ask how teachers can become involved effectively at an appropriate level.

Rationale for Teacher Intervention

Teachers should not be fearful of trying to assist children's positive response to stress. They are often the most significant adults in a child's life, other than the parents. Actually, there are educationally sound reasons for becoming involved.

First, stress interferes with learning. While it is difficult to quantify the impact of stress on children's academic achievement, for some children stress is a major impediment to learning and almost all children occasionally are diverted by the effects of stress. To the extent that the child can respond effectively to the stressors in her or his life, the more attention that child can give to performing school-related tasks.

Second, stress interferes with classroom management. This book is not intended to offer a system or strategy for classroom organization and management. The focus is on the individual child, while management systems must eventually focus upon the group or class. Yet children's responses to stress may include both acting out and withdrawal, both of which are maladaptive and are not conducive to effective classroom management. To the extent that the child can develop adaptive or positive responses to stressful events and situations, classroom management is enhanced.

How does the teacher, who is not a therapist, become appropriately involved in assisting children with stress? One need not be a therapist to be therapeutic. Teachers have regular extensive and intensive contact with the child over an extended period of time, giving them the opportunity to observe and interact with the child and to observe and have an effect upon changes in behavior over this extended period. The teacher usually has a great deal of information about the child and the family and may know a number of things about the child the parent does not know. If a positive child/teacher relationship exists, the child is likely to view the teacher as a potential source of support.

The teacher observes and works with the child in the larger social context of the school, while the therapist usually does not have the opportunity for this broad, real-life perspective. This offers the teacher the opportunity to utilize the social context in planning and implementing multiple intervention strategies for assisting children, as well as to assess their effects.

The teacher, because of traditional role expectations, can identify and select specific stressors for intervention, whereas the therapist would try to assist the child with the entire set of life problems. Effectiveness in responding to specific stressors may have a positive effect on the larger set of life's problems. For example, a teacher may help a child who is regularly bullied on the way to school by generating effective responses to the bullying. Removing a stressor, such as being bullied, from a child's life is therapeutic. If the bullied child is also known to be depressed, the teacher's intervention is still appropriate. The therapist, viewing the same bullied, depressed child, would be more likely to focus upon the child's personal motives for being bullied.

One final word about teaching and therapy. Most teachers are aware that they are not trained as therapists and so have been reluctant to enter a potential therapist-patient relationship with a child. While this concern is understood, it is important to realize that many things done by those other than therapists can be therapeutic. Well-meaning and informed teachers are not likely to do psychological harm to children by showing concern for their feelings and problems and by attempting to assist them in understanding and developing positive responses to stressful events and conditions in their lives.

2

A Stress-Intervention Model

• Mrs. Stevens teaches second grade in a mid-sized urban school where many of the children come from homes with single parents and limited financial income. When school started in September, Mrs. Stevens noted that Wanda often came late to school and was frequently disheveled and dirty in her appearance. Otherwise, Wanda did not stand out as a problem, nor was she exceptional in a positive way either. In most respects, she was like a number of schoolchildren who just melt into the woodwork and go unnoticed. However, she was repetitively late and noticeably less clean than the other twenty-four children in the class.

After a couple of weeks, which Mrs. Stevens used as a kind of yardstick for settling down or getting adjusted to school, she decided to confront Wanda in a nonjudgmental way about being late, while not saying anything about her untidy appearance. Wanda usually came in about 9:00 A.M., at a time when the rest of the class members were already involved in their reading groups. This gave Mrs. Stevens a few minutes to ask Wanda why she was late.

Wanda replied that she had overslept and added that she had had no time for breakfast and was hungry. Mrs. Stevens decided to get a small carton of milk and a few saltines from the lounge next door. With only limited encouragement Wanda began to talk as she ate her food. She told Mrs. Stevens that her parents were divorced last summer, her mother worked at night, and she, Wanda, had a younger brother. At this point, since there was a class to attend to, Mrs. Stevens told Wanda in a positive, concerned way that they could talk again later.

Mrs. Stevens neither prejudged Wanda nor her mother, initially or later, as further information was revealed during short moments of the day. Wanda's mother worked as a waitress at a night club and occasionally needed to take her two children with her to work. The children did not get much sleep there, and they usually arrived home around 1:30 A.M. When the alarm clock sounded in the morning, Wanda was expected to get up and go to school—a lot of independence to ask from a seven-year-old, Mrs. Stevens thought.

Mrs. Stevens was empathic with these events, since she had two children of her own and knew from her own experience what it was like to care for a home and have a job too. She was also aware of her better fortune than Wanda's mother: Her children were older, and she had a husband who provided financial and emotional security. In fact, Mrs. Stevens had interrupted her teaching career for a while so she could give more attention to her two children. None of these options were available to Wanda's mother.

In a few days, Mrs. Stevens arranged to see Wanda's mother at school at the end of the day. The events reported by her daughter were confirmed. Wanda's mother knew it wasn't good to take her children to work, but she didn't know what else to do. Mrs. Stevens suggested that she might like to discuss with the school social worker her needs for nighttime child care.

Shortly after the incident in which Wanda was confronted and given a morning snack, Wanda's four-year-old brother, Louis, appeared with Wanda at the classroom door, without breakfast and hungry. Mrs. Stevens noted that Wanda was on time for school. Mrs. Stevens fed them but began to think of some other way to solve the problems of getting up in the morning, having breakfast, and arriving at school on time.

Mrs. Stevens decided to encourage Wanda to get up a little earlier in the morning, feed herself and her brother, and leave in time to walk to school. This would help her mother, who was tired from working at night. As Wanda took these steps, Mrs. Stevens asked her to tell her how they were working and praised her for her independence. Now, instead of being gratified by being fed by the teacher, Wanda was praised for her independence. She also identified with the teacher through feeding herself and her younger brother, just like her teacher had done for her. Later on, Mrs. Stevens was able to add taking a shower or washing herself in the morning as an added expectation. Again Wanda received praise for doing these activities by herself.

In this example, several stressors in a second grader's life came to the attention of her teacher through a number of behavioral indicators—tardiness, disheveled appearance, and hunger. Most children of Wanda's age can eat breakfast and arrive at school on time, presenting a neat and clean appearance. *Atypical* behaviors such as hers can be indicators that something stressful may be going on in the life of a child. A *change* in a child's behavior from what is usual may also be a behavioral indicator of life stress. An example might be a child who is usually on time and dressed neatly for school who develops a pattern of tardiness and unkemptness. The evidence of either type of indicator—atypical or changed behavior—merits further investigation of a child's life situation.

Wanda was a direct source of information at school, and her mother was a confirming source. The settings included the classroom and an after-school meeting with the mother. Accomplishing such an investigation was well within the responsibility and time constraints for a teacher. It seemed natural for Mrs. Stevens to do so.

A behavioral indicator may lead to the identification of a stressor in a child's life, that is, a clearly identified life event that causes an emotional disequilibrium. In Wanda's situation there were, over some period of time, multiple stressors that probably had a cumulative influence—marital discord, divorce, one-parent family, financial difficulties, and mother working. Various instabilities and lack of structure were the consequences of such events, including increased expectations of children, inadequate child supervision, and poor sleeping habits.

Given the existence of stressors and their consequences, what interventions might be appropriate for a teacher to attempt? Reactive interventions can be directed at altering stress events and their consequences. Teacher decisions should be made through a process called *initial appraisal*, which involves utilizing available information and obtaining more if necessary in order to decide if a stress event is present, whether a child's behavioral reactions justify intervention, and what type of intervention might be applicable.

Mrs. Stevens' appraisal went something like this: First, she knew that Wanda's school behaviors merited investigation. This investigation led to the identification of multiple stressors in Wanda's life. Mrs. Stevens fed Wanda and was empathic with her when the stressors were identified. Asking only a few questions, she explored the situation and actively listened to Wanda's replies.

The teacher discovered potential stressors from Wanda's present and past life, as well as a number of consequences of these stressors. She assessed the events as having a significant impact and as probably responsible for Wanda's behavior. Wanda sensed her teacher's concern and interest as well as her compassion for her mother. It was relatively easy to establish trust, so much so that Wanda brought her younger brother for breakfast a few days later. This was certainly not anticipated by Mrs. Stevens, but she responded by feeding both children, recognizing that they had, after all, arrived on time for school! She also knew that some additional intervention, other than providing breakfast, was needed. She took a chance by encouraging Wanda to get up earlier in the morning to feed herself and her brother. This was presented as a positive expectation and one that might solve her problems and those of her brother, and also be of help to her mother, who was tired in the morning from having worked the night before.

As Wanda began to practice this assigned responsibility, she was praised by her teacher, receiving positive attention for independent behaviors. Instead of being fed by the teacher, Wanda could identify with her by being responsible for feeding herself and her brother. Later on, as appropriate, Mrs. Stevens made additional expectations, asking Wanda to take a shower or wash herself and lay out her clean clothes at night. She tried to alleviate the stress situation by suggesting to the mother that she could obtain childcare assistance. Mrs. Stevens continued to monitor Wanda's behavior and eventually was able to discontinue special attention and rewards, because of Wanda's progress.

Understanding Behavior

The preceding vignette presents a variety of behaviors—those of Wanda, her brother, Wanda's mother, and Mrs. Stevens. Three aspects of understanding behavior are involved: description, inference, and interpretation. *Description* is readily observable and objectified, such as "being late." *Inference* is not directly observable but is based on description and involves the assignment of meaning. An example is learning that Wanda gets up early, feeds herself and her brother, and arrives on time for school, a set of behaviors to which we assign a meaning: "independence." *Interpretation* is concerned with the observer's cognitive step of making a cause-effect behavior statement. An example might be the interpretation that Wanda identified with the teacher and because of that was motivated to feed her younger brother as well as herself.

A teacher should be firmly grounded in observation and description before inferences are made. Most of the time teachers will operate at descriptive and inferred levels of behavior. Interpretation often is not necessary.

Identifying Life Events as Stressful

In the vignette about Wanda, atypical behaviors led to the discovery of life stress. There are many other examples of behavioral indicators in children, either atypical behavior or behavioral change. These will be presented in more detail in chapter 4. There are also times when a teacher knows that a potentially stressful event has occurred in a child's life; then the teacher's task is to determine whether the event is stressful.

As indicated previously, stress is defined as a clearly identifiable external life event or chronic life situation (stressor) that causes a psychological disequilibrium in a child sufficient to result in a behavioral reaction (response). The behavioral reaction, like the behavioral indicator, is either a change in behavior or an atypical behavior whose onset can be associated in time or otherwise causally related to an environmental event or condition.

As is true with adults, stressful events in children's lives are composed, to varying degrees, of actual events combined with fears, fantasies, and real or imagined consequences. Let's look at some more case examples.

• A true story is told about a five-year-old boy, referred to here as Scott, who was engaged in an eyeball-to-eyeball confrontation with his mother before dinner. She wanted him to take a bath, but he wanted to watch television. The more Scott protested his mother's request, the more angry she became, and she eventually shouted a command: "I told you to go upstairs, now!" The boy stamped his foot and ran out of the house, picking up his older brother's baseball bat as he left. With all his force he smashed it against a telephone pole by the sidewalk. At that very instant all the lights in his house and on the block went out. Several hours later he was found by concerned parents and police, terrified and cowering in a neighbor's basement, convinced that his rageful act had darkened the whole street. He didn't know that the entire East Coast of the United States was without lights. It was the blackout of 1965 (Kliman, 1968).

Hitting a telephone pole in an outburst of anger became a stressful event for Scott since it was linked in time with a chance happening, a blackout. The link resulted in a causal connection in Scott's mind that his angry action was responsible for the lights going out. In his view his anger was powerful, dangerous, and frightening. He hid out of fear and concern that he might be punished. Such thinking and feeling are not unusual for a five-year-old child. Scott illustrates how a relatively minor life event can take on a stressful dimension because of unique individual circumstances and personal meanings.

• Mort, age eight, was convinced that he knew that a pedestrian overpass was going to fall. When it did fall, he was sure that if he had been more insistent with his parents and teachers, he could have prevented children from being hurt. For not doing so he felt guilty and personally responsible for a tragedy and its consequences.

The story of Mort's premonitions was pieced together by his teacher and a school nurse after a school accident in which a truck struck an overpass as children were going to school in the morning (Blom, 1981). His premonitions first began after a series of happenings the previous summer. Mort's maternal grandfather died and his family traveled to Iowa for the funeral. On that occasion, his grandmother insisted that Mort touch grandfather's body so that he would know that he was dead. After the funeral, the family returned home via Chicago, where they visited the King Tut exhibit.

Upon arriving home, Mort collected his favorite toys and placed them beside his bed so that if he died they would be buried with him. He also began to play out an event in his back yard, where he repeatedly built an overpass with lumber and made it fall. During this time, he told his parents that he was sure the overpass nearly completed next to his school was going to fall and people would be hurt. His parents reassured him over and over again that this would not happen. When school started, Mort shared his concern with Miss Rogers, his new first-grade teacher. Understandably, she also reassured him and heard nothing more from Mort until the school accident happened ten days later.

It was on a Friday morning in September at 8:30 A.M. when a truck with a forty-ton crane was moving south slowly on the major thoroughfare in front of Mort's school. The crane failed to clear the pedestrian overpass, shearing it partly off its foundation on the east side of the street. Between sixteen and twenty-five children were on the overpass at the time; six of them fell fifteen feet to the pavement below and were rushed to nearby hospitals.

The accident was observed by over 100 children on the school playground and was heard by the principal, teachers, and auxiliary staff inside the school. Mort had just walked over the overpass and was on the down-side ramp near the school playground when the accident happened. Not only had he predicted the accident, but he had been spared while six others were seriously injured.

Mort and the other children on the school playground were quickly brought into the school building by the teaching staff and grouped in the hallway according to their classes. This was done to shield the children from the postaccident happenings and confusion outside the .school and to provide them with some immediate support from a familiar adult (teacher), classmates, and schoolmates. The parents of the children were contacted and asked to take them home.

Mort's mother was at home and immediately rushed to school to take Mort and his younger sister home. The teacher recalled that Mort's mother was especially distressed and talked about how Mort had been afraid that the accident would happen. In those hectic moments, the teacher only vaguely recalled having reassured Mort that the skywalk would not fall. Mort's father later recalled that the thirty minutes it took him to reach his children from work were the longest moments in his life. The family then went home for what turned out to be an emotionally upsetting weekend for Mort and his parents.

The next school day was Monday, and Mort was not there, but the teacher had her hands full dealing with the other children's questions, anxieties, and excitement. She finally got some classroom order and then structured a period for sharing of feelings, questions, and answers. Afterwards, the children were encouraged to resume some of their usual class routines. In the afternoon, Miss Rogers asked the children to draw pictures expressing their feelings about the accident.

It was not until school was out that Miss Rogers remembered to call Mort's mother. When she did, the mother reported that Mort was having a hard time sleeping, had bad dreams, and in general was depressed and anxious. He did not want to go to school, and she had not forced this issue. Miss Rogers expressed her concerns and indicated that she would have a member of the school staff contact the mother to see if help could be provided. The mother was grateful and expressed eagerness for the help.

Two days later, the school nurse made a home visit and obtained current and background information about Mort and his family. The maternal grandfather's death was identified as a potential stressor and the subsequent events of King Tut's tomb and Mort's nighttime anxieties were also identified. It was felt by the school nurse and the teacher that the complexities of fate, situational circumstances, and at-

tached meanings warranted that Mort be referred to the accident intervention team for further evaluation and possible psychotherapy.
Mort returned to school in a few days and participated in further
classroom processing of the school accident. The team did recommend
therapy, which Mort received for a number of months. He eventually
recovered from his emotionally traumatized condition.

In retrospect, the grandfather's death was identified as a stress event
in Mort's life. It may have been aggravated by the grandmother forc-
ing Mort to touch his grandfather's dead body so that he would con-
ceptualize death as final and irreversible. Probably Mort had not yet
assimilated these events when he was exposed to a compounding circumstance: the observation of King Tut's tomb and its artifacts.
When he returned home, his grandfather's death and the tomb probably became interwoven in his thoughts, as evidenced by his placing
favorite toys beside his bed at night in case he died in his sleep.

It was shortly thereafter that the skywalk became a focal point of
Mort's anxieties and self-concerns. His inner disturbance was displaced onto a circumstantial event, the building of a skywalk near his
home, which was being completed in time for the opening of school.
Mort became concerned about an accident in which others might be
injured, rather than himself. His concerns became a conviction and
therefore a predictable event that could be prevented or controlled if
adults would only listen to him. Their reassurance that the overpass
would not fall did not help Mort. In his play, he repeated over and
over again a skywalk accident, with no resolution to his dilemma.
Mort's struggles with anxieties about death, circumstances of fate, and
the unpredictable resulted in a traumatic emotional reaction that took
more than support, reassurance, and catharsis to overcome.

Scott and Mort were two children who shared the concept of personal causality for fateful events that took place in their lives. Scott,
age five, believed it was his action (hitting a telephone pole with his
brother's baseball bat) that caused all the lights to go out in the
neighborhood. Mort, age eight, believed in the power of his thought
to predict an accident; he felt responsible when it happened. These
examples of magical thinking, psychic causality, and egocentrism are
evident in the cognitive development of children as discovered by
Piaget (Elkind, 1974).

Reactive Interventions by Parents and Teachers

With Scott, reactive interventions by his parents consisted of explanations that the coincidence of his hitting the pole and the lights going out was a chance occurrence and he was not responsible for darkening the neighborhood. The blackout was the result of a power failure unrelated to the bat incident. These explanations were reassuring and corrected his personal causality belief. The boy resumed his usual normal behaviors by bedtime.

With Mort, various reactive interventions by his parents and teacher were ineffective in mitigating his painful behavioral reactions, expressed in his thinking, feeling, and action. Mort remained inhibited and fearful, maintaining his belief of personal responsibility for the skywalk accident. It took many months of psychotherapy before restoration of emotional stability and comfort was achieved.

Developing a Stress-Intervention Model

In the previous descriptions of different events in the lives of Wanda, Scott, and Mort, a number of common elements can be recognized. These elements have to do with how parents and teachers identify and analyze stress in children and make decisions about helpful interventions. Experiences with elementary school children and teachers reveal similar elements in a wide range of stressful events that happen in children's lives.

The similarity of elements suggests that a conceptual model for understanding stress can be developed that provides a way for teachers to identify, appraise, and intervene in feasible and appropriate ways. Such a model must be readily applicable to children in classroom situations. The stress-intervention model presented in this chapter seems to meet these needs. Many elementary school teachers have reported favorably on its use in their classrooms.

Let's consider Wanda, whose atypical behaviors were first observed by her teacher and suggested the need for further inquiry about possible stressful life events, her current status, and background information. The teacher obtained information from various sources, mainly Wanda, her brother, and her mother. This led to the identification of a number of stressors, including marital discord, divorce, single-parent family, financial difficulties, and the mother's type of employment. The teacher's appraisals of Wanda's behaviors, stressors, and past and current family status led to a number of interventions: encouraging Wanda to talk, feeding her breakfast, expressing positive concern, making a positive alliance with Wanda's mother, encouraging independent behavior and identification with the teacher, and providing praise. The teacher monitored Wanda's behavior over time and made appropriate changes in and additions to her interventions. When Wanda's behavior stabilized, teacher interventions were discontinued. These activities can be categorized and organized as shown in table 2.1.

With Wanda, behavioral indicators were noted first and led to the identification of stressors, but, in Scott's and Mort's cases, potential stressors were identified first. With them, the next step was to determine the actual stressful impact of potential stressors by obtaining

TABLE 2.1   *The Stress-Intervention Model as Applied to Wanda's Case*

Elements of the Model	Application in Wanda's Case
Settings and sources of information	Wanda, her brother, and Wanda's mother at school
Behavioral indicator(s)	Atypical behavior--late to school, dishevelled, dirty
Stressor(s)	Divorce, single-parent family, financial difficulties, mother's type of employment
Current and background status	Marital discord, consequences of divorce
Teacher appraisal	Child behaviors, stressors, past and current family status
Reactive intervention(s)	Encouraging discussion, feeding breakfast, giving positive concern, making positive contact with mother, encouraging independent behavior, providing praise
Monitoring child behavior	Changes in and additions to intervention, decision to discontinue

information about behavioral reactions, that is, changes in behavior or atypical behaviors. The elements of the model progress as follows:

> Settings and sources of information
> Stressor(s)
> Behavioral reaction(s)

Subsequent steps of status evaluation, appraisal, intervention, and monitoring are similar to the case for Wanda, discussed previously.

The elements of the stress-intervention model can be arranged as shown in the flowchart in figure 2.1. The steps that precede "initial teacher appraisal" are information-gathering functions that are related to identification and analysis of stress. Initial teacher appraisal

FIGURE 2.1   *Stress Intervention Model*

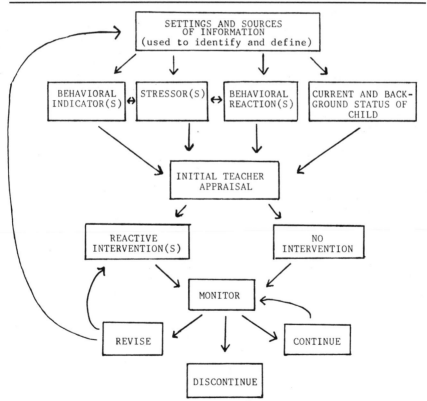

involves performing this analysis, that is, synthesizing information about stressor(s), behavioral indicator(s) or reaction(s), and the current and background status of the child. The model's purpose is to facilitate decisions about intervention. The teacher may decide not to intervene. If intervention is decided upon, the type of intervention must be chosen. Specific interventions by the teacher are labeled "reactive" since they follow or come after (react to) an identified stressor with accompanying behavioral reaction. The teacher monitors child behaviors and the effects of reactive intervention(s) and makes further decisions to continue, discontinue, or revise the interventions.

In the remaining chapters, elements of the model are described separately in greater detail. Examples and suggestions are presented that will help teachers apply the model in their work with children in the classroom.

3

Stressors and Their Characteristics

Consider three immediate life events: a twelve-year-old boy approaches an eleven-year-old girl to ask her to go to the movies with him; a fourth-grade girl brings home a report card with all A's, and her father immediately calls her grandmother to share the news; at a school performance in which she is expected to do quite well, a nine-year-old girl drops her baton four times. Then also think about two long-term life situations: the parents of three children quarrel almost every evening because of the father's heavy drinking; a seven-year-old boy's father is chronically ill and has had surgery twice in the last two years, and more surgery is scheduled.

These three events and two situations are all potential stressors, even though they seem to vary in seriousness and importance. Without knowing how the children responded in these five examples, we cannot know if they created stress. But it is known that these are the *kinds* of events and situations that may create stress when they occur. If they cause psychological disequilibrium in the child so that a behavioral response to the event or situation results, there is stress. The focus of this chapter is on those events and situations.

Articles on stress in the general population and specifically on stress in children abound in the popular literature of the past few years. The magazines for the homemaker tell how stressful life is for our children (Diamond, 1982), which events in the lives of children are reported to be the most troublesome (Carro, 1980), and how children are abused in our schools (Hentoff, 1980). According to an Associated Press syndicated article (Springer, 1983), elementary school children in Derby Line, Vermont, were involved in a stress management program to help them understand and resist stress in their lives.

These are examples of the many articles alerting us to stress in the lives of children; their cumulative impact leads to the conclusion that stress is inevitably bad and that it should be greatly reduced if not eliminated; or failing that, our children should be taught various body relaxation, verbal meditation, and other physical measures to overcome the negative effects of stress.

Hans Selye, one of the pioneers in researching stress, believes that stress is a natural and essential part of life (Selye, 1956). The important issue is whether stress is stimulating or retarding to growth. Put another way, for any particular child, stress may be a challenge or a threat. All children face potential stressors. Through their efforts in responding to these stressors, children can learn appropriate adaptive behaviors so that such experiences can lead to personal development and growth.

Acute and Chronic Stress

Stress can be thought of as having a time dimension, and stressors have somewhat the same characteristic. Stressors sometimes take the form of an environmental *event*; in such cases the term "acute" is often associated with them. *Situations* or *conditions* can also be potential stressors. The term "chronic" is often used to characterize this type of stressor. So the language that is usually employed to discriminate between these two kinds of stressors is *acute stress event* or *chronic stress situation*. Since children's responses to acute stress events may be somewhat different from their responses to chronic stress situations, it is helpful to distinguish between the two when possible.

The nature of the onset of the stress is often useful as a distinguishing characteristic. The onset of chronic stress is usually more gradual, develops more slowly, and tends not to be associated with a single traumatic event. Acute stress occurs rapidly and is usually associated with a single event, occasionally of crisis proportions.

The duration of the stress tends to be quite different for chronic than for acute stress, with chronic stress usually being long term in nature. Acute stress, or at least the stressor that precipitates acute stress, is often short term, sometimes diminishing as rapidly as it occurs. When it continues beyond some arbitrary time interval, perhaps a month, acute stress becomes chronic.

Now return to the beginning of this chapter and consider the five potential stressors discussed there. Which seem to have the characteristics of acute stress events? Which seem to be chronic? If you look at onset and duration as criteria, the first three seem more acute than chronic. The boy-girl movie episode, the high academic achievement with the accompanying attention from father, and the baton dropped four times in one performance all happened relatively suddenly, and the stress event did not last very long. The parents' quarreling about the father's drinking and the long-term illness of the father are clearly chronic situations rather than single events.

Sources of Stress

Just as with adults, many if not most of the potential stressors in the life of a child are generated out of their relationships with others. One important exception to this generalization has to do with the stress that occurs in body experiences such as illness, injury, or impending surgery. Body experiences are an important source of stress in children and will be discussed later in this chapter and in subsequent chapters.

For the very young child, human relationships are centered in the immediate family: a parent or parents and older and younger siblings. As a child grows older, the circle of human relationships enlarges rapidly and so do the potential sources of stress. As the environment of the child grows wider, so also do the sources of stress broaden. The potential stressors, which for infants and toddlers are limited largely to the family and the home, expand to include the peer group and nonfamily adults at about age five, when the environment begins to include the neighborhood and the school.

Potential stressors are events or situations that are commonly thought of as having negative characteristics, such as pain, loss, failure, humiliation, and threat. However, positive life events such as success, high achievement, and accomplishments may be stressful if they cause emotional disequilibrium and result in behavioral response.

It has been the authors' experience that teachers may overlook school—and themselves as an important part of school—as sources of potential stress. Because of their understanding of children and their humane inclinations, teachers can produce a list of potential stressors in a wink. To their collective and individual credit, teachers generally are sensitive to the problems caused to children by such events as moving to a new home, the loss of a parent, or the birth of a new baby brother or sister. But until school as a source of stress is called to their attention, teachers may overlook the problems caused by such stressors as parental pressure for academic achievement, teacher pressure to conform to classroom rules or regulations, or low-level teasing of a child by classmates.

Yamamoto's (1979) study of middle-grade children shows that stressors associated with the school were reported by children to be about as troublesome as those stressors not associated with school. For example, "being held back a year in school" was reported to be about as troublesome as "having parents quarrel" and much more than "going to the dentist."

In addition to the potential stressors of the home, school, and neighborhood, as the growing child moves into the larger community, relationships with others in the community also become potential stressors. Meeting and learning to relate with peers outside the neighborhood, competing against sports teams from other parts of town, and being sent to the store alone to make a purchase for the first time are examples of the potential stressors in this larger community.

As mentioned earlier, in addition to the potential stressors that develop from human relationships, there are potential stressors that exist in the child's body experiences. Some of these are developmental, exemplified by the child being at one end or the other of "normal" growth patterns, that is, being the shortest boy in the class or the tallest girl. There is an obvious interactive effect in this example. Being the shortest boy may be stressful in and of itself, but it can certainly be made more stressful by peer teasing. The onset of puberty is another example of a potential stressor that is developmental in nature. It happens to all children, and associated body changes in the context of similar changes in peers can be stressful when comparisons are made among peers about the timing and extent of body change.

Illness, surgery, injury, and disability are examples of nondevelopmental potential stressors that are rooted in body experiences. Both their physical and emotional significance will influence the nature and intensity of their impact on children.

The physical environment, together with human relationships and body experiences, can be stressful to children. The effects of fires on school children have been documented (Perry & Perry, 1959). Blom (1980a) has studied the psychological aftermath of a tornado and the impact of a school accident (Blom, 1981).

There are personal psychological experiences that are a source of stress. These may include scary dreams, getting lost, being suspected of lying, being caught in a theft, losing a personal possession, death of a close friend, and an outstanding personal achievement.

Sources of stress (stressors) have been presented in a number of ways in this chapter. Human relationships, body experiences, personal psychological experiences, and the physical environment are all sources, and these are found in the context of the home, school, neighborhood, and larger community. These sources and contexts usually interact with each other in various ways.

Types and Severity of Potential Stressors

Those human service professionals, including teachers, who work regularly with children seem to have a good idea of the kinds of events and situations that create stress in children. The research by Coddington (1972) on "life change events" in children was referred to in chapter 1. He developed a set of life events for each of four age groups: preschool, elementary school, junior high, and senior high. He had human services professionals give each event a weighted score in terms of severity. These events ranged from the death of a parent, being the most severe, to becoming a full member of a church, being the least severe. Other events such as the divorce of parents, death of a brother or sister, birth of a brother or sister, moving to a new school district, and beginning another school year were included.

Yamamoto (1979) identified twenty events and situations as potential stressors in the lives of children. Through direct inquiries with children he was able to arrange the stressors according to severity. The children rated a new baby sibling as least severe, while losing a parent was rated as most severe. Losing a game, getting lost, being sent to the principal, a poor report card, and going blind were among the twenty events.

Blom, Cheney, and Snoddy (1982) asked classroom teachers and other school professionals to identify those events and situations that often cause stress in children. Table 3.1 is a listing of fifty-one potential stressors. The major contexts of these stressors are school and

TABLE 3.1 *Potential Stressors Identified by Teachers*

1. School tests	27. New school
2. Alcoholic parent	28. Relations among school staff (strike)
3. Divorce	29. Adverse publicity about school
4. Teacher behavior	30. Tension between parents/school staff
5. Mental illness in family	
6. Death of parent	31. Losing something
7. Peer pressure	32. Homework
8. Holidays	33. Tardiness/absence
9. Special events (birthday)	34. Punishment/rewards
10. Sports competition	35. Rules and regulations
11. Parents' loss of job	36. Confusion about directions at school
12. Moving from school to school	
13. Physical abuse	37. Inappropriate school placement
14. Psychological abuse	38. Relations with peers
15. New family member (birth)	39. Being labeled
16. Poverty	40. Teasing
17. New parent	41. Parental pressure to achieve
18. Academic pressure	42. Nuclear threat
19. Accident/injury	43. Fears about fires, tornados
20. Physical appearance	44. Noise levels
21. Undiagnosed physical problem	45. Religious indoctrination
22. Chronic illness	46. Child/teacher conflict
23. New teacher	47. Family life style
24. Reassignment of teacher	48. Criticism
25. Substitute teacher	49. Dentist/doctor visit
26. Student teacher	50. Sibling competition
	51. Ethnic/religious discrimination

Source: Blom, Cheney, and Snoddy, 1982

home with a few dealing with the neighborhood, larger community, body experiences, and personal biological experiences.

While the Coddington (1972) and Yamamoto (1979) stressor lists were weighted in terms of severity, the list in table 3.1 is not so weighted. If duplicate items are eliminated from the three lists combined, the total of potential stressors is reduced from 107 to 87. Table 3.2 identified potential stressors that arise according to location. Of these 87 stressors, 30 happen at home, 26 in school, 8 in the neighborhood, 6 in the larger community, while 17 could occur in any location or more than one location.

In analyzing the potential stressors in terms of their sources, the number that come from human relationship (69) is much higher than those coming from body experiences (10), personal experiences (5), and the physical environment (3). It is apparent that most potential stressors for children originate in their human relationships.

Stressors may be classified in other ways. There are, for example, predictable and unpredictable stressors. One may prepare for the stress of elective surgery, but an accident inflicting pain and injury is quite unpredictable. Although it would seem that the impact of unpredictable stressors might be acutely stressful, in reality the responses to the two kinds of stress by individuals can be expected to vary widely, depending upon the circumstances of each situation. It may be possible, of course, for teachers and parents to intervene more effectively in preparing children for predictable stress. The routine attention to fire drills for schoolchildren is a case in point. While no one can predict when a fire may occur in school, there is certainty that such an event will be stressful as well as dangerous, and that preparing children to cope with such an event is only prudent. People who commonly deal with dangerous and unpredictable events, as in military service or police work, are prepared through educational programs to react almost automatically to the dangers that they may face. Heroism, though hardly routine, may in fact be more often a consequence of knowing what to do in life-threatening situations rather than the result of being "pumped up" with altruistic impulses. In any event, there are many educational efforts devoted to training people to react to stressful situations in effective ways.

Stressful events clearly vary in severity. Few would doubt that a child's encounter with an adult molester would be more intensely stressful than the loss of a hard-fought basketball game. This distinction may blur, however, in looking only at the immediate, short-lived

TABLE 3.2 *Potential Stressors of Elementary Age Children, by Location*

HOME (N=30)

Death of a parent

Divorce of parents

Marital separation of parents

Death of a brother or sister

Jail sentence of a parent

Marriage of a parent

Discovery of being an adopted child

Increase in number of arguments between parents

Birth of a brother or sister

Increase in number of arguments with parents

Change in father's occupation requiring absence from home

Mother beginning work

Jail sentence of parent for 30 days or more

Serious illness requiring hospitalization of brother or sister

Addition of a third adult to the family

Loss of job by a parent

Death of a grandparent

Brother or sister leaving home

Pregnancy in unwed teenage sister

Change in parents' financial status

Decrease in number of arguments with parents

Decrease in number of arguments between parents

Alcoholic parent

Mental illness in family

Special events (such as birthday)

Psychological abuse

Poverty

Having regular chores at home

Sibling competition

Physical abuse

SCHOOL (N=26)

Failure of a grade in school

Move to a new school district

Beginning school

Suspension from school

Beginning another school year

Giving class report

Not making 100

Ridiculed in class

Sent to principal

Poor report card

Wetting in class

Tests

Teacher behavior

New teacher

Reassignment of teacher

Substitute teacher

Relations among school staff

Adverse publicity about school

Relations among parents and school staff

Homework

Tardiness/absence

Child/teacher conflicts

Confusion about directions in school

Inappropriate school placement

Being labeled

Parental pressure to achieve

TABLE 3.2 *(Continued)*

NEIGHBORHOOD (N=8)

Death of a close friend	Peer pressure
Change in acceptance by peers	Family life style
Losing a game	Going to the dentist
Picked last on team	Becoming a full member of a church

LARGER COMMUNITY (N=6)

Religious indoctrination	Nuclear threat
Authority figures	Serious illness with hospitalization
Ethnic/religious discrimination	Becoming involved with drugs and alcohol

ANY LOCATION (N=17)

Outstanding personal achievement	Getting lost
Suspected of lying	Going blind
Caught in theft	Accident/injury
Criticism	Undiagnosed physical problem
Sex relationships/questions	Physical motivation
Acquiring a physical deformity	Noise levels
Having a visible congenital deformity	Losing something
	Punishment/rewards
Scary dreams	Holidays

emotion that may be vented as youngsters respond to these two kinds of stressors. Escaping with one's life may override the sense of peril as the child thinks of the adult's advances, while the more trivial misfortune of losing an important game is viewed as a calamity from which there is no recovery. The point is that the severity of the stressor is not necessarily an indicator of the impact of the stressor on behavior.

The impact of stressors is further complicated by cumulative effects. Stressful events often have consequences that are themselves stressful. A child's lie that is found out may continue to be a source of mistrust, rancor, and guilt revisited well beyond the time when it should have been forgotten. Sometimes unrelated stressors occur in rapid succession, amplifying the impact of stressors that, experienced individually, would be quite tolerable. The well-worn phrase, "a run of bad luck," is an adult expression describing this interactive stress. A child may read more into successive events and be unable to dismiss them as unrelated. The boy whose dog is hit by a car soon after he has been moved to a lower reading group and kept after school for fighting with a classmate may connect the events and conclude illogically that the dog's misfortune is punishment for his own misbehavior and incompetence.

Children are also the victims of multiple stressors that *are* related. The family in which alcoholism leads to economic privation, social ostracism, and family discord places its children in a chronically stressful environment that may make the more typical stressors of school and neighborhood particularly burdensome. It is inspiring to observe that there are children who bear up well under such multiple adversities. More typically, of course, children endure such circumstances without collapsing but without reaching their full potential either. Sadly, there are a few who fail even to defend themselves against these multiple stress events.

Common Group Stressors

Occasionally children in school experience a common stressor as a group. Examples of such group stressors may be a tornado disaster, a series of child molestations by an unknown person in the neighborhood of a school, or the discovery of a serious contagious disease among children who attend the school. The impact of a group stressor is obviously complicated and varies in the intensity of effect and response among the children and adults who are involved. Important aspects of the impact of group stressors have been described by Blom (1981) as experiences in which the "predictable world becomes unpredictable." The disorder, the perceived loss of control over events, and the feelings that trusted adults have failed to shelter them are components of the general sense of loss of a dependable environment, which children express through their behaviors.

Eight-year-old Mort's personal response to the skywalk collapse was described in chapter 2. This event is an example of a group stressor.

It is used here to illustrate the range of behavioral responses that were observed and the steps taken by the school to deal with the responses of children and their parents to the disaster. Recall that the skywalk collapsed as some children were playing nearby and others were crossing it on their way to school. Sixteen to twenty-five children were on the walkway, and six of them were injured. A large number of children on the playground witnessed the accident, as did a few adult passersby.

In the aftermath of the accident, the school principal called Blom, a child psychiatrist, to express his concern about meeting the needs of parents who wished to have assistance in dealing with their children's continuing reactions to the disaster. A team of professional caregivers was mobilized, consisting of parents and a nurse, a psychologist, a teacher, and a social worker from the school staff, as well as several psychiatrists and psychologists from the Department of Psychiatry at Michigan State University and the Tri-County Community Mental Health Center. This planning group convened to consider a great number of concerns and questions that had already been raised in connection with the incident.

Parents expressed concerns about the need for realistic information and the clarification of rumors, what to expect from their children when the injured returned to school, how to respond to questions about death that some of the children were asking, what traffic safety measures would be instituted, and what to advise children to do when the skywalk was rebuilt and open for pedestrian traffic again.

Teachers were described as effective agents in meeting the needs of children and their parents, from the moment of the skywalk collapse and during the long aftermath in which effects of the incident were observed. Predictably, the reactions of children and adults spanned a wide range. Some showed great resiliency and resumed their familiar life patterns almost immediately; others reacted with startle to sirens and other loud noises and complained of unusual dreams and sleep disturbances; some of the younger children became more babyish and irritable; many were reluctant to go to school, ride the bus, or leave their parents; some developed fears of the dark, bedwetting, hand tremors, and hyperactivity; questions about death, injury, and God were common. For most children these behaviors diminished over a period of two to four weeks, yet follow-up information seven months later indicated that behaviors traced back to the accident still persisted. The teachers were aware of these behaviors and sensitive in dealing with the children who exhibited them. They encouraged children to express their feelings and helped them distinguish reality from fantasy. When class meetings were needed to allay fears, they were convened, but the teachers were careful to maintain normal expectations for children, to avoid augmenting fears and dependencies that would foster lower expectations than were necessary and helpful.

The collapse of a skywalk in a Midwestern American city is a minor calamity when compared to the horrors inflicted on children who live in the war zones of the world, and yet the responses of children to their respective stressors are similar. In summarizing his book, *Children of War*, writer Roger Rosenblatt (1983) acknowledged that, when he started his investigation, he had no idea what he would find among children of the Middle East, Southeast Asia, and Northern Ireland. Yet he discovered that, in spite of the ordeals of war, children retain their childlike characteristics. On this note it would be easy to heave a sigh of relief and reassure oneself that everything will be all right because children are tough and resilient and able to cope with whatever they confront. Some are, it is true; but, for many, help sensitively provided by caring adults is urgently needed.

Unique Individual Aspects of Stress

The labeling of stressors as severe, acute, and traumatic on the basis of external factors may be quite misleading. It is the personal meaning attached to stressors by the children who suffer them and the capacity of each individual to respond adaptively that determine the impact of stress. The capacities of children to respond are influenced by such factors as parental support, family stability, environmental vulnerability, age and stage of development, and personal attributes of temperament. Children who are able to rise above clusters of overtly stressful events and conditions encourage the belief that personal attributes may provide a kind of stress resistance. Larger numbers of children are observed to be less well defended against the impacts of stressors, however; and it is these who may be helped by teachers who will take time to understand them and prepare them for stressors that may reasonably be anticipated.

In the chapters that follow, our stress-intervention model will be developed further in the hope that it may help teachers in making the difficult decisions regarding intervention in any particular case.

4

Children's Reactions to Stress

In previous chapters we have emphasized the importance of defining stress in a clear, conceptual way, as an identifiable life event or situation that causes emotional disequilibrium sufficient to result in a behavioral response. As we have stated, two criteria must be met for stress to be present: an identifiable life event or situation (stressor) and a behavioral reaction. In this chapter the behavioral-reaction aspect of stress will be discussed from the viewpoint of expressive behavior. In the next chapter the child's response to stressors will be examined in terms of processing and outcome behaviors.

In a case example given at the beginning of the book, a third grader, Jerry Meyers, began to show less attention to schoolwork and started quarreling more with friends. This was viewed by his teacher as an indicator of a possible stressor in Jerry's life. This stressor was later identified as a contemplated family move. Thus, the two criteria for stress were met—a stressor (the contemplated family move) and a behavioral reaction (inattention to schoolwork and quarreling with friends).

In a similar fashion, Wanda, a second grader discussed in chapter 2, displayed atypical behaviors in the classroom involving persistent tardiness and being untidy in appearance, which were seen by her teacher as indicators of stressors in Wanda's life. The teacher discovered that Wanda's mother was divorced, had financial difficulties, and was working at night.

A distinction is made between a *behavioral indicator* and a *behavioral reaction*. The latter is a change in behavior or an atypical behavior that is connected in time with a *known* acute stressor or chronic stressful life situation. A behavioral indicator, on the other hand, is an expressive behavioral sign pointing to the presence of a stressor that has yet to be identified. An indicator can be a change in behavior (Jerry) or atypical behavior (Wanda) that is observed *prior* to the identification of an acute stressful event or a chronic stressful situation. Both indicators and reactions represent the response aspect of stress.

Atypical behavior consists of abnormal or unusual behaviors according to age, sex, or situational context. For example, it may be atypical for a second-grade girl to be consistently tardy and unkempt in appearance at school. A change in behavior, on the other hand, is a deviation from what is usual or typical for a specific individual child. For example, Jerry Meyers, a third grader, was described as getting along well in school, with average schoolwork and good social adjustment to peers; then his behavior changed to less attention to schoolwork and more quarreling with his friends. It also is possible for behavior to be both atypical and involve change.

Both behavioral indicators and behavioral reactions are viewed as the initial expressive responses of stress. They represent the immediately detectable behaviors activated by the emotional disequilibrium caused by the life event or situation. These expressive behaviors display a variety of forms and modes. As indicated by the children cited previously, behaviors can include quarreling, poor attention, tardiness, unkempt appearance, anxiety, nightmares, school phobia, running away, and hiding.

Domains of Expressive Behavior

Responses to stress can be clustered into a number of meaningful categories. The categories represent major behavioral domains: feeling, thinking, action, and body response. In relation to stress, children may express behavior in a single domain, or in various combinations of domains. A particular behavioral reaction such as quarreling may be categorized in the domains of feeling and action. Wanda's unkempt appearance, tardiness, and hunger fit the action behavior category, while Mort's anxiety, depression, and nightmares can be categorized as feeling. In table 4.1 some specific behavioral reactions are categorized in behavioral domains in both positive and negative modes.

TABLE 4.1   *Domains of Behavioral Reactions*

FEELING	THINKING	ACTION	BODY RESPONSE
Crying	Daydreaming	Overly compliant	Physical complaint
Temper tantrum	Distractable	Tardy	Tic
Shyness	Lower academic work	Bullying	Hyperactive
Fearful	Short attention span	Lingering after school	Headache
Lonely	Not following directions	Truant	Wetting
Fighting	Confusion	Stealing	Soiling
Low self-confidence	Overachieves	Provokes punishment	Stuttering
Sadness	Reads poorly	Teasing	Frequent use of bathroom
Shame	Poor achievement	Clowning	Clumsiness
Quiet	Not finishing assignments	Withdrawal	Well coordinated
Phobia	Nonsensical thoughts	Overly dependent	Well groomed
Overly polite	Alert	Unkempt appearance	Nail biting
Angers others	Good memory	Impulsive	Vomiting
Bravado	Concentrates	Regression	Nausea
Worry	Asking repetitious questions	Natural	Sucks thumb
Overly modest		Tolerates frustration	
Moody		Responsible	
Sense of humor		School absence	
Friendly		Overly polite	
Nightmares		Helpful to others	
Anxiety		Running away	
Depression		Hiding	
Stable mood			

Children show a variety of behavioral reactions to different types of stressful events in their lives. A group of elementary teachers in a graduate class reported a large number of stressors that they observed in their classrooms over a one-week period. These are listed in table 4.2, along with selected characteristics of the children and their associated behavioral reactions or indicators.

The eighteen stress events and situations identified in table 4.2 vary from losing scissors in the classroom to child abuse, from dropping a baton during a school performance to separation/divorce/remarriage. Those occurring with the highest frequency were illness, moving, and separation with divorce.

The range of behavioral reactions or indicators was also wide with regard to the different domains of expression. In the feeling category there was complaining about unfairness and crying, the latter more often found in younger children. Overall, most striking was the large number of action behaviors, representing about one-half of all the behavioral reactions reported. Actions such as fighting on the playground, tattling on other children, and clinging to the teacher comprise the expressive mode that characterizes children in general. In the thinking domain there was writing a gory story and attending less to schoolwork. Body responses were represented by headaches, hyperactivity, and flushing of the face.

In addition to the high frequency of action behaviors, there are other psychological characteristics of children that make them more vulnerable to stressful events and influence their behavioral reactions. These are dependency on others, limited rational thinking, a subjective concept of time, and the influence of fantasies and imagination on perception and understanding of environmental events.

Manifest, Inferred, and Interpreted Behavior

Another aspect of the expressive behaviors of children involves the observer, in this instance the teacher. The teacher often deals with child behavior from three different but related perspectives of understanding. First, there is the manifest, overt behavior of the child, most clearly generated by the child, which the observer can describe and rate in terms of strength and frequency; the observer selects and fo-

(continued on page 44)

TABLE 4.2 *Stressors and Behavioral Reactions in Elementary School Children*

Child	Stressor	Behavioral Reactions
6-year-old girl	Loses scissors in class	Wrings hands, cries easily
7-year-old girl	Anticipates doctor visit, shots	Outbursts of crying without provocation
7-year-old girl	Father looks for another job in another city, might move	Clings to teacher
7-year-old boy	Jehovah's Witness, can't celebrate Halloween	Tears, asks to leave the room
7-year-old boy	Grandfather seriously ill	Headaches, hyperactivity, flushed face
8-year-old girl	Child abuse	Headache, not wanting to go home after school
8-year-old girl	Dropped baton during school performance	Crying, stomping feet
8-year-old boy	Mother remarries, new school placement	Hits a classmate with his fist, teases other children
9-year-old girl	Mother in hospital for week	Cries easily, less attentive to work

10-year-old boy	Very small stature, failed high jump in gym	Cries, runs from gym to class, slams books on desk
10-year-old boy	Leukemia, treatment causes loss of hair, wears a cap	Reluctant to attend school
10-year-old boy	Parents separated, compete with each other for child	Fights on playground, complains about unfair situations
10-year-old boy	Frequent family moves	Wrote a very gory Halloween story
10-year-old boy	Superior intelligence, parent pressure	Uses knowledge to put others down
10-year-old boy	Father abusive to children, problem drinking	Agressive behavior toward peers
11-year-old girl	Father in hospital for surgery, chronically ill	Throws down spelling test, didn't know word
11-year-old girl	Father loses job, financial crisis at home	Withdraws, puts head on desk, does not relate to peers
12-year-old boy	Birth of sister	Tattles on other children in class

cuses on child behaviors that are considered or judged to be more salient and important.

Second, there is an inferred, covert aspect to the child's expressive behavior in which a mental process in the observer attributes meaning to or forms a judgment or impression about manifest behavior. Third, there is an interpreted aspect to the child's behavior in which the observer makes a logical cause-effect explanation for or attributes a reason to manifest behavior or inferred aspect of behavior. Interpretation requires the use of further information about the child beyond manifest behavior or about psychological theory in general.

For example, Lucy, one of the eleven-year-old girls listed in table 4.1, usually was an energetic, friendly person who related easily to peers and was well liked. Then a change in behavior occurred. Lucy became withdrawn, did not relate to her classmates, and often put her head down on her desk. Her teacher noted these changes and spoke to Lucy about them. Lucy told her that her father had lost his job and her parents were very worried about how they were going to pay the rent and feed the family.

Withdrawal, not relating to classmates, and laying her head on the desk are all manifest behaviors observable to others. From these manifest behaviors, an inference could be made by an observer that Lucy was depressed; this meaning could be attributed to the behaviors. Furthermore, based on additional information and psychological theory of depression, a reason for the manifest behaviors and inferred depression also could be stated: they have occurred because of the helplessness and loss experienced because of her father's unemployment and family financial problems. When a logical cause-effect relationship is established, the manifest behavior and inference can be interpreted.

Teacher interventions can be made using any of these aspects of understanding behavior: manifest, inference, and interpretation. Manifest behavior may be ignored or reinforced; an alternative, more desirable behavior may be encouraged, reinforced, or modeled. An inference may be communicated to a child to encourage conscious recognition and provide emotional support from a teacher. An interpretation also may be discussed with a child in order to provide insight and cognitive mastery.

The interventions selected by Lucy's teacher focused on the meaning of her manifest behaviors and on making a cause-effect connection between her depression and events in her life.

Summary

The behavioral indicator and behavioral reaction elements of the model for stress intervention have been presented. There is no behavioral difference between an indicator and a reaction; rather, the distinction is made based on what has been observed or noted first. If a change in behavior or an atypical behavior is noted first, then the term *behavioral indicator* is used. This may be a sign of the existence of a potential stressor. The teacher utilizes various settings and sources of information to explore that possibility. On the other hand, if a teacher knows that a potential stressor exists, then the task is to find out if an observable change of behavior or atypical behavior is also present; this is termed a *behavioral reaction*.

Behavioral reactions and indicators are expressive and can be categorized into four different behavior domains: feeling, thinking, action, and body response. In children, action behavior is typically more frequent.

Teachers who observe children's behaviors usually deal with them from three perspectives: manifest behavior, inference, and interpretation. Manifest behaviors are describable, visible, and directly observable. Inferences are made about behavior by the observer through assigning meaning to the manifest behavior. Interpretations by the observer consist of establishing a cause-effect explanation for manifest behaviors or inferences utilizing additional information.

5

Processing Stress

• A nine-year-old boy, Chris, was discovered with a classmate stealing from a hall locker at school. His teacher, Mr. Mullins, observed the behavior unobtrusively and brought it to the boys' attention in a private talk at the end of the school day. Chris was somewhat defiant, accusing Mr. Mullins of spying and insisting that he had not stolen anything. His reactions of anger, mistrust, absence of guilt, and defensiveness continued when the teacher indicated that the stealing justified calling his parents. Chris's classmate, John, in contrast, cried, apologized, expressed his shame, confessed having taken some lunch money, and reluctantly accepted the teacher's decision to contact his parents. John's behavioral reactions indicated to Mr. Mullins that the locker event might be resolvable and that his behaviors were probably correctable, given average parental support. In the classroom, John was liked by his classmates but occasionally needed behavioral limits set when he got out of hand. The teacher generally viewed him as well within the typical range of behaviors for boys his age.

Mr. Mullins was not as optimistic about Chris, who occasionally got into fights with other children, was reluctant to accept personal responsibility for wrongdoing, and could be surly toward authority figures. The teacher did not find him a likable boy. While Chris showed a certain level of chronic irritableness, there were also discrete episodes of negative behavior that his teacher thought might be connected with his home life. For example, the episode of stealing took place on a Monday, causing Mr. Mullins to wonder if something might have happened at home over the weekend.

After the boys were dismissed, Mr. Mullins called their parents. John's mother was appropriately upset about the stealing episode and readily agreed to a teacher conference that also included her husband. She even asked if it would be advisable for John to be present as well. When the teacher asked if she knew of anything that might be going on in John's life that might be upsetting, John's mother was silent for a few moments. She then tentatively wondered if her husband's working extra hours on weekends in his accounting firm might be affecting the family. With good reason, Mr. Mullins felt comfortable about the reaction of John's mother and looked forward to the meeting with her, John's father, and John, in a few days. In fact, Mr. Mullins recalled a time when he was a boy of ten years; his father had changed his working hours from daytime to the night shift. He suddenly remembered that he had taken some money from his mother's pocketbook and bought a candy bar. He felt some guilt in recalling the loss of money, since it had not been discovered and he never "confessed the sin." Mr. Mullins smiled and marveled at the workings of his mind.

The consequential events with Chris's parents were more frustrating. First, no one answered at Chris's home when he called twice that afternoon. When Chris returned to class the next day, Mr. Mullins felt that things were not settled between the two of them. He knew that he should have told Chris he had tried to contact his parents, but somehow Mr. Mullins was not up to doing that. He got on the school phone several times that afternoon and on the fourth attempt from his home phone, he reached Chris's mother. She was annoyed by his call, indicating that she and her husband were very busy; they had no problems with Chris at home; there was nothing stressful that took place at home over that weekend; furthermore, she didn't have time to set up a conference with the teacher and they would take care of the problem themselves. She hung up on him. Mr. Mullins was annoyed and frustrated at Chris's mother's denial, defensiveness, anger, and criticism of him. He thought that perhaps there were some kids and their parents that you could do nothing about.

At school the next day, there was a sullen silence between Chris and Mr. Mullins. During lunch break Mr. Mullins happened to be in the teacher's lounge at the same time as the school counselor. She was friendly as usual and asked him how things were going. Mr. Mullins commented about how there were some kids and families that you couldn't reach and help. The counselor picked up on his pessimistic mood and asked if he was thinking about someone in particular. So Mr. Mullins shared the story of Chris and John and their families, all the while feeling annoyed at the counselor's habit of being helpful to others. What came out of this exchange was that the counselor suggested that she try to contact Chris's mother again. Again, this was not easily achieved, in spite of the counselor's nonthreatening approach. Eventually a home visit was made and the father's episodic problem drinking was identified, along with family fighting and instability. This frequently happened on weekends with Sunday becoming hangover-recovery day rather than a time for family activities and for Chris to do things with his father. The timing of the episode of stealing on

Monday, right after an especially troublesome weekend of binge drinking, seemed significant. It required a great deal of effort by the school counselor and social worker to encourage Chris's mother to seek help for herself and for Chris and his siblings. It took several months for this to happen.

In this example, one can see how the same behavioral indicator—stealing from a school locker—pointed to the identification of stressful events in the lives of John and Chris. The similarity between the cases stops there, since the nature of the stress event, the reactions of the boys to being confronted by the teacher, their usual classroom behaviors, and the responses of their parents were quite different.

Chris in general displayed more negative action behaviors than John, such as fighting with others, being surly, and getting involved in wrongdoing. This negative behavioral style is often referred to as "acting out" or "externalization." This style represents a characteristic way a child processes feelings and events in his life. It can also be the way he deals with stress as well. Chris could be called an "externalizer." There are studies that indicate that short- and long-term behavioral adjustment outcomes are less favorable in children and adults who have an externalizing behavioral process style. They have been compared to individuals who have an internalizing response style; that is, those who respond inwardly to stress, through feelings and actions such as sadness, withdrawal, and shyness. Internalizers, as compared to externalizers, demonstrate more successful school, family, and occupational adjustments in both short- and long-term follow-up studies (Garmezy, 1970; Weintraub, 1973).

Another difference between the two boys emerged when they were confronted by Mr. Mullins, their teacher. John assumed responsibility for the stealing, expressed shame about his behavior, and stood up to the bad news and consequences. Chris, however, was protective and defensive, avoided the problem, and blamed the teacher for spying. Again, their behavioral styles were different; that is, the ways in which they processed events and behaviors were different.

Coping, Defending, and Fragmenting Processes

Behavioral styles can be identified by the way children process the content of a stress event and its associated behavioral reactions and

consequences. These processes have an outcome goal of stress resolution. Three main types of behavioral processes can be discerned:
coping, defending, and fragmenting (Haan, 1977).

Coping involves a posture of challenge or active dealing with life
events and associated feelings. In certain ways, John reflected this
posture and showed characteristics of coping such as expressing feelings, discussing events, feeling shame, accepting consequences, and
assuming responsibility for what happened (an internal locus of control) (Lefcourt, 1976).

Defending consists of an attitude of threat or protection or avoidance of unpleasant events and behavioral reactions. Chris was defensive, protective, and avoidant. He showed a number of behavioral
characteristics associated with defending, such as withdrawing, unwillingness to face consequences, blaming others, denying guilt, and
not taking appropriate responsibility for what happened (an external
locus of control) (Lefcourt, 1976).

The third behavioral process is fragmenting, in which the posture
is perceived danger (imagined or real) where neither active dealing nor
protective measures are used to deal with stress and behavioral reactions. As an example of this latter process, let us consider Pat, age
fourteen. Following surgery with anesthesia in the hospital, she became flooded with panic feelings, reported peculiar sensations in her
tongue, mistrusted nurses as wanting to hurt her, and displayed other
disorganized behaviors. Over a four-week period after hospitalization, during which time she was medicated with a tranquilizer at
home, she gradually resumed a more defending behavioral style of
inhibition, avoidance, compulsions, and rigidity. This was her more
typical behavioral style (process).

We have further developed the concepts of coping, defending, and
fragmenting from various professional literature sources (Garmezy,
1981; Haan, 1977; Murphy & Moriarity, 1976; White, 1979). In table 5.1 a list of distinguishing characteristics of these three behavioral processes has been assembled in a comparative fashion. For
example, the first entry on the list compares how feelings are man-
aged. A coping person expresses feelings with control, while a defensive person inhibits feelings and a fragmented person floods with
feeling. In the children previously discussed, Pat showed flooding,
Chris inhibited some feelings, and John expressed feelings with control. Further down the list of characteristics, the use of fantasy is
compared in the three behavioral processes. Going from left to right

TABLE 5.1 *Comparative Characteristics of Coping, Defending, and*
Fragmenting Behavioral Processes

Coping (challenge)	Defending (anxiety)	Fragmenting (perceived danger)
Expresses feelings with control	Inhibits feelings	Floods with feelings
Discusses events with others	Keeps thoughts to self	Is mistrustful of others
Reasonable, realistic perceptions	Unreasonable perceptions	Distorted perceptions
Displays caring and empathy	Blames others, is egocentric	Holds delusional views of others
Tries to master and overcome adversity	Avoids problems	Flees from problems
Exercises creative imagination	Daydreams	Private, autistic thinking
Ability to concentrate	Restricted ability to concentrate	Distractable
Displays purposeful behaviors	Shows rigid behavior	Displays ritualistic strange behavior
Acts older than age	Acts appropriate age	Acts younger than chronological age
High tolerance of frustration	Intolerant of frustration	Loses emotional control
Feels shame when standard is not met	Feels guilt when standard is not met	Feels anxiety when standard is not met
Uses problem-solving approach	Just does minimum	Sees no solutions
Oriented to present needs	Oriented to past needs	Confused about past and present
Feels pull to the future	Feels pull to the past	Has confused perspective
Demonstrates flexibility	Demonstrates rigidity	Is disorganized
Has internal locus of control	Has external locus of control	Has no locus of control
Feels confident, hopeful	Lacks confidence, is pessimistic	Holds negative self-view and outlook
Seeks out information	Withdraws and avoids information	Ignores information
Considers alternative choices	Limits choices	Makes random choices
Considers consequences	Denies consequences	Does not consider consequences

in the table, we see that coping involves exercising creative imagination, while defending is characterized by daydreaming and fragmenting involves private, autistic thinking. Last on the list is consequences, where coping involves considering consequences, defending involves denial of consequences, and fragmenting means one does not even consider consequences.

In addition to the distinguishing characteristics listed and compared in table 5.1, children's perceptions of stressful events and their behavioral reactions differ in qualitative ways. These qualitative distinctions are given in parentheses at the top of table 5.1. If the child's view consists of challenge, then behavioral processes actively attempt to master environmental and behavioral events. On the other hand, if the child perceives events as fraught with anxiety or inner apprehension, then protective, cautious, and conservative behavioral processes are involved, which characterize defending. Another extreme view of environmental and behavioral events is one of perceived danger, more than apprehension. It may be realistic danger, but it can also be irrationally perceived danger. Behavioral processes under these circumstances fail to deal actively with the problem, nor do they help the person to overcome it or protect themselves from stressful events and behavioral reactions.

For any given child, the behavioral processes of coping, defending, and fragmenting are on a dynamic continuum, as shown in figure 5.1. Since these processes are multidimensional in their characteristics, overlapping patterns may exist for a child under different conditions at different points in time. The overlap creates mixtures of processes, such as coping and defending; coping, defending, and fragmenting; and defending and fragmenting. The four behavioral outcomes (stress resistance, adaptation, maladaptation, and psychopathology) also are on a dynamic continuum, with the two extremes being special forms of adaptation and maladaptation. The only overlapping outcome pattern of practical significance is that involving adaptation and maladaptation, where there are mixed patterns.

A specific child will not always cope with a stressful life event. There may be times during stress events and situations when defending or fragmenting will exist. Mediating variables of a personal or environmental nature will influence how events are perceived, responded to, and processed.

In the previous example of fourteen-year-old Pat, who perceived hospitalization, surgery, and anesthesia as dangerous and life threat-

FIGURE 5.1 *Relationships Between Process and Outcome Behaviors*

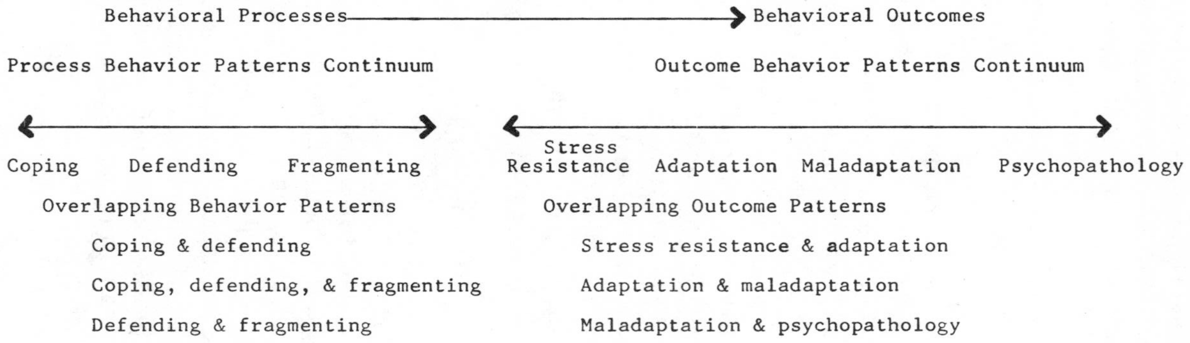

Behavioral Processes ─────────────────────────▶ Behavioral Outcomes

Process Behavior Patterns Continuum   Outcome Behavior Patterns Continuum

| Coping | Defending | Fragmenting | | Stress Resistance | Adaptation | Maladaptation | Psychopathology |

Overlapping Behavior Patterns

  Coping & defending

  Coping, defending, & fragmenting

  Defending & fragmenting

Overlapping Outcome Patterns

  Stress resistance & adaptation

  Adaptation & maladaptation

  Maladaptation & psychopathology

ening, following these events there were fragmenting behaviors at first. Slowly, over four weeks, her processing behaviors became more defensive and therefore more organized; however, she did not progress to coping behaviors.

Examples of children with different overlapping behavioral process patterns can be given in relation to the chronic stress situation of divorce.

- Magna, age nine, lived with her mother and younger sister. Her parents had been divorced two years before. Magna's teacher described her as fitting well into the classroom. She was outgoing and thoughtful of others. The only behavior the teacher questioned was her being an overachiever, seemingly to please her teacher and mother.

One interpretation is that Magna was primarily coping (displaying caring and empathy, purposeful behaviors, and problem solving) but showed some evidence of defending (demonstrating overly high standards and some rigidity).

- George, age ten, was an only child, whose parents had been divorced the previous year. He was quite close to his father, in spite of unremitting arguments between his parents. Six months before, his father had moved to another state and was considering a second marriage. George's teacher spoke of him as being somewhat withdrawn and a slow worker academically. George had difficulty in reading but did exceptionally well in math. He seemed to feel guilty about his difficulties in learning.

George seemed to show more defending behaviors (guilt when standards were not met, lack of confidence, withdrawal, rigidity) than coping (exceptional performance in mathematics).

A third example, Sheila, age eight, illustrates fragmenting behaviors.

- Sheila was the third of five children in a family in which the father was a problem drinker. After several separations, her parents had divorced three years before. At the present time there were financial problems and her mother had to work to obtain an adequate family income. Sheila frequently expressed fears to her teacher that she didn't know who she was. She forgot the names of the other children in the class. In the classroom, she usually worked slowly, by herself. When the teacher tried to get her to talk more about her problems, she would deny that she had any. Occasionally, Sheila would have an angry temper tantrum without prior indication of distress. The teacher was concerned about her and referred Sheila to the school social worker for further evaluation.

The Relationship of Process to Outcome

Process-oriented behaviors result in various behavioral outcomes on a continuum from adaptation to maladaptation in responding to stress, as indicated in figure 5.1. There is a means-end relationship between process and outcome. Coping usually results in a successful adaptive behavioral outcome, but this is not always the case. Defending often is associated with less adaptive behavioral outcomes, while fragmenting usually, but not invariably, will lead to maladaptive psychological responses. The relationship between process and outcome is not always predictable because there can be dynamic changes over time in the nature and intensity of stress, shifts in the domains of behavioral reactions, altered mediating factors, and spontaneous or planned interventions.

Taking one extreme of the adaptive-maladaptive outcome continuum, adaptation consists of stress resolution (mastery) characterized by stable typical behaviors, body wellness, competence, and life satisfaction. There is a special form of adaptive outcome that is called "stress resistance" or "resilience." While it is found in a relatively low percentage of children, its importance lies in pointing to the special adaptiveness of a few at-risk children who master adverse situations, handicaps, and multiple stressors. These coping children may have special individual endowments, but they also learn coping behaviors and achieve special psychological competencies and satisfactions. They will be discussed in greater detail later in the book.

At the other extreme of the adaptative-maladaptive continuum, maladaptation consists of failure to resolve stress, psychological disequilibrium, unhappiness, somatic symptoms, and dysfunctional behaviors. There is a special maladaptive extreme of psychological disturbance, sometimes called psychopathology. It affects a relatively small percentage of the child population who may have special vulnerabilities. Survey studies of large populations have estimated the percentage of psychologically disturbed children to be in the range of 8 to 15 percent (Gould, Wunsch-Hitzig, & Dohrenwend, 1981; President's Commission on Mental Health, 1978). Disturbed children often need special school and community services. Stress occurs in their lives, and it may be possible for teachers to assist such children in a limited way. The limited application of the stress-intervention model to emotionally disturbed children may be a focal point around which problem-solving efforts can be mobilized. A disturbed child may master a particular stress event, or sometimes a child's behavior may become generally more adaptive.

Outcome Studies on Stressors

Large-scale studies on the outcomes of specific stressors on children point to the existence of this adaptive-maladaptive continuum. There are limitations to some of these studies, however, because they do not clarify the nature of stress conditions, individual and environmental factors, and mediating variables. Blom (1958) reported a four-year follow-up of 150 children who were exposed to a predictable stress of tonsillectomy and adenoidectomy. Of this group in the age range of three to fifteen years, (mean age of six to seven), twenty-five (17 percent) had severe postoperative psychological reactions that lasted several weeks but only four (6 percent) developed psychological disturbances. Most of the other children had mild and temporary behavioral reactions, while twelve children eventually showed a noticeable improvement in their adaptive behavior. In some, this seemed to be a consequence of improved health status, but in others the hospital experience was perceived as a challenge and was responded to in a coping way.

In a study of an unpredictable event, a school accident, Blom (1981) found 19 percent of families had one or more members displaying psychological disturbances two to four weeks later. Seven months afterward, only 3 percent of the children attending the school appeared to have lingering psychological trauma. Eighty-one percent of the families who appeared to resolve the stress experience did so within four to six weeks. There were four children who displayed behaviors of courage, mastery, and heroism. Again, these children were a special group of copers; they represented about 3 percent of the population of the school.

Summary

In this chapter, we have shown how stress events may be perceived, responded to, and processed over time with different behavioral outcomes. Examples of individual children and studies of populations of children point to particular personal and environmental variables that influence the processing of stress and its behavioral consequences. Three behavioral processes can be discerned: coping, defending, and fragmenting, each with distinguishing characteristics. However, they are on a dynamic continuum so that mixtures of processes occur for any given child at different points in time. Processes are also related to various behavioral outcomes that include adaptation and maladaptation.

6

Identifying Stressors

Teachers are apt to observe behavioral indicators of stress most often at certain times and locations. These times and locations often have common characteristics, which will be discussed a little later, but first consider these examples.

• Lisa was in her third week of student teaching in a kindergarten in a suburban school district. Mrs. Soloman, her supervising teacher, asked Lisa to conduct the morning sharing time with the class. Bridgett shared her new doll with the class. Then Mike was about to tell about his older brother receiving an award for a theme he had written, when Jordon interrupted Mike by saying, "I want to show you my back," whereupon he pulled up his T-shirt and turned his back to Lisa. Jordon's back was a terrible sight; he had obviously been beaten with a belt or switch. Jordon said, "My dad beat on me because I broke the new lamp in the livingroom." Lisa felt very close to being ill; she also realized she was about to lose control of her class. Feeling very uncertain about how she should deal with the situation, Lisa asked Jordon to put his shirt down and promised she would talk with him later. Jordon seemed satisfied with that and complied. Sharing time went well after Mike reminded Lisa that he was interrupted by Jordon and he didn't get to tell about his brother's award. After a long talk with Mrs. Soloman about what should be done, it was decided that Lisa would seek Jordon out sometime during the morning, when they could talk privately.

• Middle school industrial arts teacher Bryan Adams knew that Tom Biddle had been troubled about something ever since Tom had entered the woodworking class two months earlier. Tom's woodworking skills were okay, but he approached his projects in a somewhat sullen, isolated, and usually silent way. When Bryan approached Tom, he would physically pull away and, when possible, actually move away. He was also unresponsive to verbal approaches. This pattern was repeated many times, but on one occasion when Bryan was commenting on a project Tom was completing, a slightly different response occurred. Bryan said that he particularly liked a small wooden box that Tom was finishing and indicated that he was sure Tom's father would also like it. Tom replied that his father wouldn't care, that he wouldn't even show it to him, and that his parents did not live together. Showing empathy and listening actively, Bryan found out that Tom hated "the old man," that Tom's father was mean and used to beat Tom and his younger brother. When the father visited on weekends Tom and his brother would stay away from home. Following this exchange, Bryan and Tom developed a friendlier relationship, presumably based upon the sharing of a chronic stressful situation.

• Mark was a substitute teacher for the months of January and February for a third-grade class. He felt he was an effective teacher with most of the children in the class, and that generally he was very well liked. Some of the mothers of the children had a small party for Mark in his classroom on the last day he was there. When the school principal called Mark in late April to see if he could resume his substituting for the same class, Mark was delighted. It was a chance to teach and earn some money, and he felt he knew the children. It would be a pleasure to complete the school year there. The children seemed happy to have Mark back with them. Generally, things went along very nicely, but one thing bothered Mark. Anne seemed to have changed since the last of February. Earlier in the school year, she seemed quite responsive to Mark. She was a strong student and continued to do excellent academic work, but she just didn't seem as friendly and open as she had been. On the playground, where she had sought him out before, Anne seemed to avoid Mark. When he would speak to her, Anne would answer in a terse manner and not volunteer any more than was asked. Not knowing what else to do, Mark finally approached Anne at recess when she was sitting in a swing alone. Mark asked if something was wrong and why she didn't talk with him like she used to. Anne only mumbled something about things having changed but would say no more. Mark finally indicated that he hoped they could still be friends; he said that, if Anne ever wanted to talk with him, he would be available. The next day Anne found a time to talk with Mark privately and told him she didn't want him to go away when he left last February. She was sure he would go away again, just as her father had last Christmas. Mark assured Anne that he enjoyed being her teacher and that he would stay for the remainder of the year. He also said he was sorry that her father had left her mother, and reassured her that her father loved her. Anne didn't respond, but during the final few weeks of the school year she seemed to adjust to her father's absence.

These three examples are presented in this chapter to illustrate a point. Signs of stress—behavioral indicators or reactions—occur constantly during the school day. Changes in behavior and sustained unusual (atypical) behavior often have some important meaning. Teachers can learn to be alert and sensitive to them without measurable alteration of their role as "teacher." It simply takes a certain "tuning in" to children's concerns and a lot of practice.

If a teacher is aware that there is a specific potential stressor in a child's life, the task becomes one of monitoring the child's behavior to look for changes. Knowing where, when, and how to look can be extremely useful. If the teacher observes a behavioral reaction—that is, a change in behavior or a sustained atypical behavior—available sources of information must be tapped to identify the stressor, if one exists.

Settings and sources of information about stressors take many different shapes and forms. In the example of Jordon's beatings by his father, the information came to Lisa, the student teacher, through a regular class activity, sharing time. She wasn't looking actively for signs of stress, so when she learned what was going on in Jordon's life she was startled. Stressors sometimes show up in this way.

Tom Biddle's problems with his father were revealed to Bryan Adams through a discussion of Tom's schoolwork. Bryan was not trying to find out the specific problems Tom was having; rather, as teachers often do, he was simply trying to encourage Tom and get to know him a little better.

Anne's reactions to her father's leaving the home were discovered because Mark noticed a decided change in her behavior between February and May. He used the informality of recess time to approach Anne in a way that allowed her to come to him later and express her concern.

School Settings

There are several times during the school day when activities are characterized by a lower level of teacher supervision. These times include recess, coming to and going home from school, before and after school in the classrooms and halls, lunchtime, and various daily transitions. Children may be more inclined to "be themselves" during these times of less teacher supervision, allowing relationships with their peers to be quite revealing. Likewise, there are places in the school where supervision is less intense, including coatrooms, halls, and the gymnasium.

Stressors and reactions to stressors are often revealed during times when the school itself adds potential stressors to the child. These times include test-taking and competitive situations in classrooms, the gym, and the playground, such as spelling competitions, relay races, and choosing sides for a game. If the child is already experiencing stress, the addition of school-related stressors may be enough to cause the child to respond negatively. Pressures to conform to classroom rules and standards of behavior, school policies, and peer group norms can also have an additive effect on the stress the child is experiencing.

Holiday observances in the classroom and school seem to have elements of cumulative stress also. Halloween, birthday, and Valentine's Day parties all have the potential for creating stress in children. Competition with peers for attention, a change in regular school routines, uncertainty about the unknown (a mother dressed up as a witch, for example), and other factors may also contribute. In addition, there may be less certainty on the part of the child about the rules for behavior during these observances, which may be reinforced by the teacher, who may be less willing to enforce rules during these times. All this can lead to some rather unusual behavior, though it may not necessarily be the result of any out-of-school stressors.

One other area deserves mention as having a particularly high potential for revealing stress in the lives of children. This may be characterized as those times when the child is especially influenced by the home setting, such as before school, after school, just before and after holiday periods, Fridays and Mondays, and even the first days in the fall and the last days of the year in the spring. These are the times when a child may be more apt to respond negatively to the stressors of the home and family, so a teacher might want to be particularly attentive for signs of change in behavior or sustained atypical behavior.

Sources of Information

The most obvious source of information about stress in a child is the child. Much of the preceding discussion about settings and times that are likely to be the most revealing of stress has to do with those places and times in which the child is apt to be a good source of information. There are many instances when the child wants to share problems and when the teacher may be the recipient of this information. If the teacher sends the child signals of willingness to listen, the likelihood of receiving information increases.

On occasion, the schoolwork of the child will reveal the presence of stress. Changes in the quality of schoolwork, usually abruptly but sometimes gradually for the worse, may be indicative of stress. The kinds of school assignments that encourage the child to be creative sometimes reveal the presence of stress in a child. An analysis of children's artwork or creative writing may even suggest the nature of the stressor and the way the child is responding to that stressor.

School pupil-personnel records (cumulative folders) can be a source of information about the stressors that have been present in a child's life in the past. These records occasionally suggest why a child is responding in a given way to a stressor. A child whose father has been out of work on numerous occasions and whose mother has been able consistently to provide for the family during these periods is probably less adversely affected than a child whose father has been out of work for the first time, for example.

Teachers who are careful observers of children's behavior in the classroom report that some children behave differently around teacher-parent conference time, even though their academic achievements have been satisfactory. The changes seem to be related more to the child's concern that the parent will reveal something about the home that will embarrass or shame the child. For this child the parent-teacher conference can take the form of a stressor. Parents and siblings may also reveal useful information to the teacher in general conversation. A mother's remark about the way her third-grade child acts toward the new baby in the family may be very helpful information for the teacher who has been trying to understand for a month or so why the third grader has been demanding so much attention. Jerry Meyers, the boy described in chapter 1, was expecting to move out of town with his family at the end of the school year. It was only after Mrs. Meyers told the school principal of the upcoming move that the teacher was able to associate Jerry's rather maladaptive behavior to a specific stressor. Consequently, the information the parent shared with the principal was of great value, once it got to the teacher.

Brothers and sisters who are exposed to many of the same stressors are excellent sources of information about each other. Unfortunately it is usually somewhat difficult to gain information from this source. Children are cautioned not to "tell all you know" at school. Shared stressors may lead to stress in every child in a family, even though the behavioral responses may be very different. Variations in responses among siblings can be helpful in identifying stress in the child who internalizes, that is, keeps much of the response inside. If a brother or sister externalizes or acts out, this may be of use to the teacher of the quiet, internalizing child.

Other school and nonschool professionals are also sources of useful information in some instances. A level of confidence must be established between the teacher and other school professionals (counselor, school nurse, social worker, principal) so that shared information about a child will be used in helpful, caring ways, rather than as grist for the school-community rumor mill.

Classroom Climate

The classroom teacher is a very significant person in the life of a child. Over one-fourth of the child's nonsleeping hours, for five days a week, nine months of the year, are spent in a rather intensive relationship with this adult. In chapter 1, the rationale for teachers' involvement with the problems of their students was presented, so it will not be repeated here. What teachers need and often want to know are techniques for involvement. Specifically, without disrupting normal routines and academic learning tasks, how do teachers make themselves available and approachable for pupils, so they can feel enough trust to be able to share information about specific stressors in their lives? One kindergarten teacher we know sets aside a certain period each day when her pupils know they can approach her about anything they want. Other teachers regularly schedule short conferences with every pupil, to talk about both the teacher's and the pupil's agendas, which provides a good opportunity for personal matters to be discussed and yet does not disrupt regular classroom procedure. A teacher who wants to establish a caring relationship with children will need to develop his or her own way of communicating to them that "I am interested in you; you can trust me not to betray your confidence; I'll help you if I can."

7

The Child—
Present and Past

The stress-intervention model advocated in this book depends on acquisition of information about a child. Much of the information is acquired through observation of the child's behaviors. Some is acquired through contact with parents, peers, and other sources within the school community.

Generally, the information that comes to mind first is current. Teachers are not in the habit of thinking about students in terms of their histories, although sometimes they do. Thinking historically about children creates an important mindset for teachers that helps them to provide positive learning and supportive environments at school. Some teachers currently believe that knowing too much about a child may result in a negative bias and interfere with developing a new start or a positive, corrective school experience. This belief derogates the professional capacity of teachers to assess appropriately, for educational purposes, the past and current status of children. It is important to be aware of historical thinking that is negative, such as when a teacher persists in looking at a child in the context of past positive or negative experiences with siblings and fails to see the child's own attributes. The desire to compare a child with family members may blind one to seeing the individual, who frequently stands alone in responding to life events.

Sources of Information

The stress-intervention model calls for an appraisal of the child before intervention decisions are made. The appraisal process requires knowledge of the child's background as well as of current status. Background information can be acquired through observation, especially if the relationship between teacher and child has been a long one. Background information is also gleaned from parent-teacher conferences, other professionals, records of social agencies, conversations with children, and teachers who have had past associations with the child. School records may help but often are quite skimpy in this era of increasing privacy rights.

Acquaintance with a child over time provides constant and cumulative information that is routinely available to teachers. Perhaps the best—and at times, overlooked—source of information about a child is direct conversation. One teacher obtained the following information by talking with Jim, a six-year-old boy known to be suffering from a brain tumor.

• Before the tumor was discovered, Jim told of having severe headaches and pounding in his head because of the pain. The first hospital he was taken to found nothing, but the second found a tumor as large as an egg and surgically removed it. The doctors were surprised that he had survived the surgery. The boy's black skin was, at the time, undergoing a change in pigmentation.

Jim talked of wanting to be Superman and having money with which he could buy a car for his mother. When asked what he liked most, he said "being alive." He talked much about his mother but disclosed that his father was unemployed and that he wanted his father to take him fishing. Asked about his friends, he listed many and included his teachers among them. He thought school was fun except that it required staying indoors too long. He said he wanted to be a "head doctor" or a teacher when he grew up. He worried about his mother dying and seemed preoccupied with talk about pain. He had expected the hospital to be fun but found it bad, especially his recollections of the surgery itself, which he said was performed under local anesthesia. After the surgery he felt "free" but was fervent in saying that people shouldn't drink or smoke because God doesn't approve. He spoke of praying for another child who was in the hospital with a brain tumor but who died.

A somewhat awestruck teacher talked with Jim's mother to clarify both the realistic events described by him as well as the meanings he gave to them. It was found that he had had a brain tumor removed by surgery, but under general anesthesia. His symptoms of headache and pounding were relieved by surgery, but there was ongoing concern about recurrence of tumor growth. Medical treatment and follow-up care were continuing.

Inferences can be made that these events represented an immediate and future death threat and also a threat to his body integrity. The interpretation could be drawn that he compensated for these threats through fantasies of being Superman and someone with power to buy his mother a car; he also referred to the importance of people seeking God's approval as a way of assuring life survival.

Knowing this information about this remarkable boy was helpful to his teacher in understanding his behavior. A change in his behavior would not likely be overlooked by the informed teacher, and the search for a potential stressor might be less complicated. A teacher who is well-informed about a child's background should have little trouble in gaining the confidence of parents or in collaborating with them in selecting a form of intervention.

Recommendations that teachers acquire and use information about the background and current status of children are not intended to imply that teachers should involve themselves in intensive child studies that might interfere with and go beyond their teaching responsibilities. The expectation is that teachers will collect information about all their students routinely and unobtrusively, because doing so informs their teaching decisions. When changes of behavior in individuals occur or when potential stressors are known to have occurred, the information routinely collected about the affected child becomes even more useful. In some cases the intervention decision may be to refer the child to other professionals who are in a better position to assist. Information is the basis for that decision.

Mediating Variables

In any potentially stressful situation there are mediating variables that may minimize or exacerbate the impact of the stressor, influence behavioral reactions to stress, and alter the processing and outcome of stress events. Mediating variables are those personal and environmental attributes that, taken together, cause potential stressors to have varying and at times unpredictable effects on different individuals. Put more simply, what is stressful for one child may not be stressful for another, and the impact of a potential stressor on one child may also vary from one time to another. Mediating variables usually explain these differences.

Children in great numbers are exposed to the potential stressor of parental divorce. Observation by a teacher will confirm that the impact of divorce varies widely, as gauged by the behavioral reactions of children. Consider the case of twelve-year-old Rick.

> • Rick's father announced without prior warning that he was leaving home. Rick reacted quite dramatically by becoming sullen and depressed. He slept a lot. He stopped working at his school activities and failed to carry through on commitments such as his swim team membership, which he had previously loved. He often feigned illness and was uncharacteristically open about verbalizing his feelings. Previously he had been popular with his peers—friendly, outgoing, and aggressive. Following the divorce he withdrew from associations with his classmates and sought the attention of adults. Far from being outgoing and aggressive, he became lethargic, uncaring, and unassertive. The change in his behavioral characteristics was unmistakable.
>
> Among the many environmental conditions with which Rick lived, two other events in addition to the loss of his father may have exacerbated the situation: His older brother quit high school and his mother began dating other men. His mother's relationships with men were particularly resented by Rick and invoked a discernible anger that was visible even in the context of his general state of depression.

It is not possible to predict what the impact of divorce would have been in the absence of the two additional mediating variables, but the impression of interested observers was that the two factors adversely affected Rick's ability to recover from the negative behavioral patterns that developed after the divorce of his parents. This is an example of how mediating factors can have interactive effects.

The range of reactions of fifty elementary schoolchildren who witnessed the grisly murder of a father by his twenty-three-year-old son on a residential street illustrates how one acute stressor may impact individual children in a variety of ways (Dallas, 1978).

> • Stunned at first, the children displayed a number of different reactions as time elapsed and the incident became a part of their thinking. Flashbacks, doubts, anger, disbelief, anxiety about their failure to act,

and concerns about the safety of their own lives were among the emotional responses identified by psychological caregivers who worked with the children. The principal of the elementary school mobilized the teachers and the special services personnel to become involved with the students. With the skills and cooperation of the teachers, a supportive environment developed in the school, permitting feelings to be expressed freely, without adult judgments. Children's perceptions were not denied. On the second day following the event the parents were invited to a meeting at which experienced psychologists offered suggestions for dealing with questions and behaviors that already had emerged at home or that could be anticipated.

Parents mentioned such behavioral symptoms as whining, crying, mood swings, aggression, daydreaming, fear, hanging on to the parent, thumb sucking, carrying a blanket or a stuffed toy, vomiting, headaches, stomachaches, and unwillingness to go to school. Parents were advised to make weekend plans that would put them in close touch with their children through family activities and to get children back to school as soon as possible by means of carpools or planned groups walking together over routes that would avoid the scene of the incident. As the children became desensitized, they were encouraged to go back to their old patterns of getting to school. Thinking even further ahead, psychologists urged parents not to send children to summer camp but to substitute family vacations that might tend to strengthen family ties and avoid behavioral regression over the summer.

The report of this incident (Dallas, 1978) does not include long-term effects on individual children or an evaluation of the effectiveness of procedures that were used. It does, however, verify the idiosyncratic reactions that children exhibit as a result of a shared stressor. While it is possible to disagree with some of the suggestions given to parents, the report provides an example of practical action instigated by a school staff and practiced cooperatively at school and at home. The personal and environmental variables that pertain to each individual may be cited hypothetically in accounting for the different response patterns of the children.

Another mediating circumstance is that recurring, predictable stressors may lose their stressful impact over time through a desensitization process. One remarkable child living in an environment of economic deprivation and lack of parental nurturance was able to deal with his mother's regular mood swings by withholding information from her that he judged to be "upsetting" until the "time was right" to tell her. A second, more generalized example is related to parental unemployment. Children whose parents are regularly unemployed may learn to deal with the changes in family life and the economic deprivation that accompany unemployment without apparent distress, but children unaccustomed to out-of-work parents often exhibit marked changes of behavior.

Mediating variables have been referred to as "personal" and as "environmental." In the personal category such factors as sex (boys are consistently more vulnerable to stress), chronological and developmental age, school achievement, temperament, handicapping conditions, IQ, and previous responses to stress seem to influence the impact that a stressor might have on an individual. Environmental variables include the influence of family sensitivity and support; family structure and dynamics; parental dominance and expectations; social, academic, and psychomotor experiences at school and home; peer influences; "at-risk" conditions; role models for learning behavior; socioeconomic circumstances; cultural mores; and opportunities to develop interests and skills that might offer alternative ways of responding to the immediate environmental influences.

The personal meaning of a stressor to an individual is the result of a complex interaction of the effects of a variety of personal and environmental variables, allowing for a range of behavioral reactions. A child with enough stable self-esteem, for example, may view a stressful event as a challenge and respond positively to it in spite of an array of personal and environmental factors. Children with handicapping conditions sometimes accept their disabilities as challenges to be overcome and therefore perform at levels beyond expectations.

School as a Particular Mediating Variable

School and the influence of a caring and skillful teacher may be an organizing factor in the lives of children who come from at-risk environments. Something as simple as the stability afforded by school may have a beneficial impact on the child whose home environment is without stability. Social dynamic factors in schools may also make a difference. A study of inner-city schools in London, England (Rutter, Maughan, Mortimore, Ouston, & Smith, 1979) identified particular schools that seemed to counteract negative family and neighborhood influences. Children in these schools had higher academic and social achievements and lower failure indicators than children in other schools. The successful schools were distinguished by greater visibility and feedback on student academic performance and by more consistent student behaviors such as fewer school absences and less tardiness.

• One nine-year-old named Anthony (Morris, 1982) came from a home environment that placed him at risk for a number of reasons. The youngest of nine children, some of whom he was not able to name, Anthony lived with his mother, whose history of psychological and emotional problems was reflected in her violent anger and hostility. Anthony's father had died a few years prior to the time of this report, but he still expressed sorrow over the father's absence. The mother's anger at the father for having died and left her with "all of these children" to raise was a source of confusion for Anthony. It troubled him to hear his mother, whom he cared for, reviling his father, whom he missed.

The family lived in poverty. They had only recently moved from a house that had no windows, electricity, water, or central heat. On several occasions they slept at friends' homes because of rats in their own home. Anthony's clothes typically were ripped, ragged, and unclean, and many times he came to school wearing girls' blouses and pants. Food was scarce, resulting in many meals missed.

Although he was two years below grade level in academic achievement, Anthony expressed enthusiasm for school. This is in contrast to the attitude of his mother, who was very much against his placement in special education and wrote letters threatening to keep Anthony out of school. She refused to allow him to participate in school activities such as bowling and swimming, even though Anthony wanted to participate. Amazingly, he expressed his disappointment by asking the principal and his teacher to keep working on his mother to let him participate; he expressed great joy when his mother was finally persuaded to relent.

When his brother smashed the box of crayons that Anthony had received for Christmas, he was upset but accepted his brother's action without recrimination. When home life was particularly stressful or when his clothes were clean, he would seek out his teacher to share his sadness or his joy with her. Functioning below grade level, he attacked his schoolwork with enthusiasm and spoke proudly of progress he was making toward a goal of being integrated into a resource room for part of the school day.

In the face of all of these adversities Anthony maintained several positive qualities: (1) he was able to accept circumstances which he could not change; (2) he sought out trusted adults to talk through his problems; and (3) he maintained a positive self-concept. Under the circumstances that were described, Anthony is a survivor—a "coper," if you will. But what might have happened in the absence of the school and a caring teacher? No one knows, but it is not unreasonable to think of the school as a positive mediating variable that had a great deal to do with Anthony's ability to accept the other adversities with which he was confronted. The teacher who listened and conveyed respect and concern probably made a difference; however, the teacher had this impact because Anthony had personal strengths that enabled him to talk about his troubles and his joys.

8

Deciding to Intervene

Lisa, the student teacher described in chapter 6, did not know what she should do when Jordon pulled up his T-shirt and showed his bare, beaten back during show-and-tell time. When Jordon's back was exposed, Lisa was immediately confronted with a set of problems. What could she do to help Jordon? How were the other kindergarteners in the group reacting to Jordon's display? Was she going to lose control of the group? Was Lisa going to be able to control her own emotional responses? Would what she did help Jordon, or would it cause him more problems than he already had? In asking Jordon to pull his shirt down and in going on with show-and-tell activities, Lisa was, in effect, making a decision not to intervene at that moment. Perhaps Jordon's apparent matter-of-fact attitude is what caused Lisa not to pursue the matter at that point; or perhaps it was her uncertainty as to what the most appropriate behavior on her part might be.

This is an example of an on-the-spot initial appraisal process. Following the incident Lisa consulted Mrs. Soloman, her supervising teacher. When Mrs. Soloman asked how Jordon behaved during the event, Lisa described him as matter-of-fact. He showed little embarrassment or guilt; in a way, his back was his show-and-tell topic for the day. After assuring Lisa that she had handled the situation satisfactorily, Mrs. Soloman asked her if she wanted to go ahead with the interventions that were yet to be developed, or if she would prefer that Mrs. Soloman take over. Since Jordon had selected her to display his back to, Lisa decided she wanted to remain involved. This plan of action was mutually agreed upon. Because of the laws regulating teachers' responsibilities in suspected child abuse cases, the school principal was to be informed and her advice sought. In consultation with the principal, it was determined that the school nurse would be asked to look at Jordon's back and to examine him generally to determine if there were other symptoms of physical abuse. The principal agreed that, since Jordon had displayed his back to Lisa, she should be the one to talk with him privately about how he got the beating and to try to determine his response to it.

Initial Appraisal

This process of making a decision about whether a teacher should intervene in a potentially stressful event or condition in a child's life is termed *appraisal*. Many factors should be considered in this kind of decision. Currently, most teachers make these decisions on the spot, relying largely upon their intuition and experiences. Fortunately, these decisions made by capable and caring teachers are often appropriate and reasonable and lead to solutions or potential solutions to children's problems. We have examined the process used in making judgments about whether to become involved in the stresses children experience, in an attempt to understand and explain what teachers think and do in such situations. The hope is that what is intuitive and implicit can be made rational and explicit for other teachers and helping professionals.

The appraisal process seems to involve making three basic decisions, based upon the information the teacher has available at the time. First, does the child need help (intervention) in this particular, potentially stressful situation or event? Second, what kind of help (intervention) does the child need? Third, does the teacher have one or more intervention strategies, the time to implement them, and sufficient emotional strength available to follow through on them? Or, as an alternative to the third decision, is there another resource in the school or community available for implementing the intervention?

With teacher appraisal having as its purpose the decision to intervene or not to intervene, a number of factors can be considered. The appraisal process may, and often should, take only a short time, with the factors considered in reaching the decision coming primarily from three sources. The pertinent information on the current and background status of the child, which has been accumulated previously from various sources and has become a part of the teacher's working knowledge of a particular child, is combined with the teacher's understanding of the nature of the identified potential stressor and the child's behavioral reactions to the potential stressor.

The Intervention Decision

These three factors—current and background status of the child, the nature of the potential stressor, and the child's behavioral reactions—yield information that can be incorporated into a set of criteria for reaching the decision to intervene or not to intervene. The criteria would include the following:

1. *The intensity or nature of the potential stress event or condition.* Some events and conditions are so powerful that the teacher should assume that intervention is needed. The death of a parent or sibling is an example of an event so intense that, by its very nature, it will cause reactions that merit some type of intervention. An event such as a brief argument with a class peer might warrant a casual monitoring of the child's reaction by the teacher, with no other direct intervention.

2. *The appropriateness of the child's behavioral response to the potential stressor.* Intervention should be considered when there is a change in the child's behavior or some atypical behavior that is either excessively severe or overly minimal in relation to the response expected. An example of excessive behavior might be the child who is afraid to return to school the day after the school Halloween party because most of the children wore costumes and masks. This type of phobia may be a signal that the child is overreacting to the "frightening" costumes and masks. At the other extreme, the young child who appears his usual cheerful self after the divorce of his parents may be trying to ignore this potentially stressful event by not telling anyone at school, including the teacher. Responses like these at either extreme are often signals that some form of reactive intervention is needed.

3. *Qualitative aspects of the child's behavioral response.* Intervention usually is indicated if there is a pervasive behavioral response to a stressor affecting a number of areas of the child's life at home and at school, such as academic performance, relations with the teacher, peer relations, play activities, and relations with siblings. Moreover, if intense and unusual behaviors such as constant daydreaming, compulsively following rituals, expression of irrational ideas, flooding with feelings, or disorganized behaviors are observed, then intervention by the teacher or referral to another source for intervention is required.

4. *The duration of the stress event or situation or the prolongation of the*

behavioral responses when a stress event or condition is of long-term nature. Prolonged exposure to a stressful event may continue to have a destabilizing effect on the child. Problem drinking in the family may often fit this description. However, events that have often occurred before and have become familiar to the child may lose some of their impact. Chronic unemployment, single-parent family status, and parental separation sometimes seem to have less of a negative impact as they continue, when compared to the first time they occur. If behavioral responses to an event or condition continue to reflect disequilibrium in the child, as exemplified by chronic fearfulness, lack of concentration, or poor academic progress long after (such as six to eight weeks) an event, intervention is probably warranted. If there is evidence of increasing destabilized behavior, from a mild reaction to a more severe one, intervention should be considered.

These are four important criteria to use in reaching a decision on intervention. A consideration of these criteria may lead to the decision not to intervene in a particular stress event. For example, intervention may not be needed if the stress event has a very short time duration or is not very intense, or the responses by the child were initially appropriate for the stressor and are decreasing in intensity over time, or there are sources of support other than the teacher. It is still desirable to consider intervention if the teacher can reduce pain and suffering for the child, even though there are signs that stress is being processed in a favorable direction.

Process and Outcome Patterns

There are two other sets of factors that deserve attention in making a stress-intervention decision. These are the child's behavioral process pattern and the child's behavioral outcome pattern. The responses of the child should be considered in relation to the stress event, from a number of viewpoints. One of them, already discussed, is expressive and immediate—the child's behavioral response. It is expressive in that it reflects the psychological destabilization caused by the stressor. Another view focuses on the characteristic behavior styles or patterns that the child uses to process stress events, behavioral responses, and consequences. These behavioral processes can be characterized as coping, defending, and fragmenting. If a child, over time, shows mostly coping characteristics, such as expressing feelings with control, considering alternative choices, and trying to overcome obstacles, there is less need for the teacher to intervene except to acknowledge the child's efforts to master the situation. However, if the child does not perceive a stress event as a challenge, instead becoming anxious and displaying inhibition, lack of confidence, and low frustration tolerance (defending behavioral processes) then intervention should be considered. Intervention is even more strongly indicated if fragmenting processes such as mistrust, flooding with feelings, and regression are displayed.

The child's behavioral outcome pattern follows expression and processing and is resultant behavior. Process and outcome have a means-end relationship. Coping is usually associated with adaptation as a means of stress resolution, while fragmenting is connected with maladaptation and unsuccessful stress resolution. Adaptation and maladaptation are outcomes identifying extremes on a continuum. Adaptation consists of the resumption of usual behaviors, wellness, competence, and satisfaction. When these characteristics are present, intervention is unnecessary. On the other hand, maladaptation consists of continued psychological disequilibrium, atypical or abnormal behaviors, unhappiness, and somatic distress. Such outcomes indicate a need to intervene.

Figure 8.1 depicts the factors to be considered by the teacher in the intervention decision.

Professional Referrals

The decision to intervene may in some instances involve referral of the child and his parents to professional helpers within the school system or in the community. This is called for if the nature of the stress event is severe and/or if legal reporting is required, such as in cases of suspected child abuse. However, it is also considered when the stress event and behavioral reaction persist in spite of teacher interventions, or when ineffective behavioral processing and maladaptive behavioral outcomes become apparent. This means that the teacher may need to meet the child's parents to discuss the problem

FIGURE 8.1 *The Appraisal Process and Decision Criteria*

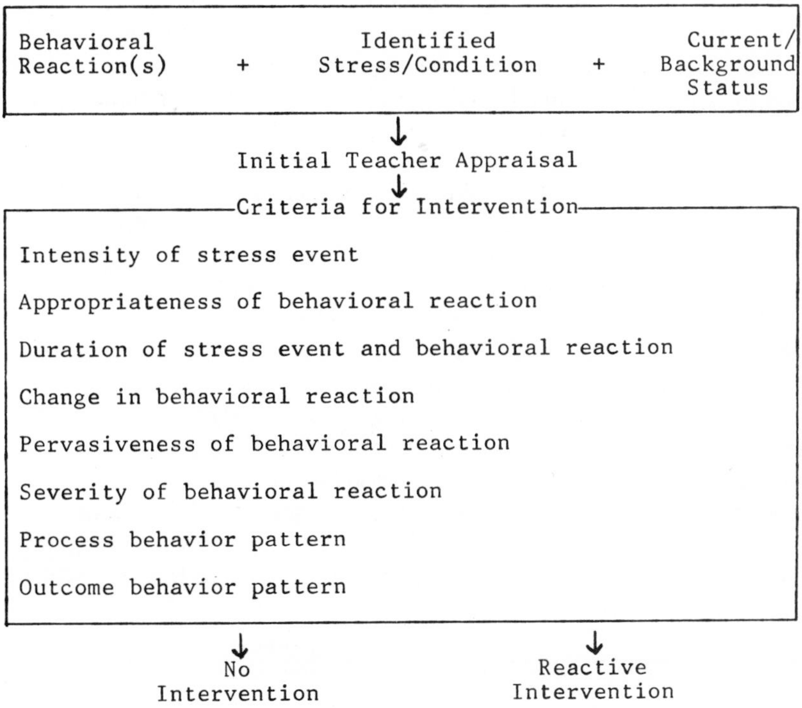

```
┌─────────────────────────────────────────────────────────────┐
│ Behavioral              Identified                  Current/ │
│ Reaction(s)     +    Stress/Condition    +        Background │
│                                                      Status  │
└─────────────────────────────────────────────────────────────┘
                              ↓
                  Initial Teacher Appraisal
                              ↓
┌──────────────────Criteria for Intervention──────────────────┐
│ Intensity of stress event                                    │
│                                                              │
│ Appropriateness of behavioral reaction                       │
│                                                              │
│ Duration of stress event and behavioral reaction            │
│                                                              │
│ Change in behavioral reaction                                │
│                                                              │
│ Pervasiveness of behavioral reaction                         │
│                                                              │
│ Severity of behavioral reaction                              │
│                                                              │
│ Process behavior pattern                                     │
│                                                              │
│ Outcome behavior pattern                                     │
└──────────────────────────────────────────────────────────────┘
              ↓                              ↓
             No                          Reactive
         Intervention                  Intervention
```

and the need for referral. Referral to resources outside of the classroom is not the end of the problem for the teacher, since the child usually will still be attending the classroom and manifesting changed and atypical behaviors. The teacher should try to stay involved and to respond in ways that facilitate the helpful interventions of others. Unfortunately, it is often difficult to obtain and maintain good collaborative communication with other professionals within the school, and this is even more difficult with agencies and professionals in the community.

Let us consider a case example where a child's behavioral reactions continued despite teacher intervention, necessitating a referral.

• Ronald was a six-year-old boy who, on the first day of first grade, refused to separate from his mother. He had had similar difficulties in attending kindergarten the previous year. His mother reported that Ronald usually protested when left with babysitters. After three months in first grade, Ronald was still being brought to school by his mother and, while separated from her, he appeared sad and lonely for an hour or so. The teacher noted that Ronald was immature for his age and seemed to remain very close to her in the classroom. Ronald's academic skills and school performance were good, but he would break out in tears when another child teased him. On a few occasions he wet in class. When issues became complex and difficult in school, Ronald would often say, "I want my mommy." The teacher was supportive of Ronald at first and then changed to being more structured and holding clear and reachable expectations. These measures were somewhat helpful, but the teacher's impressions were that Ronald was at a stalemate. Furthermore, while Ronald's mother appeared to have a stable marriage and life situation, the teacher received very little information from her about her own difficulties and the current and background status of her son. The teacher was available and receptive to the mother, but she felt she did not want to pry for further information. Clearly, the mother herself was still involved in trying to separate from Ronald, without knowing how to accomplish it. The teacher decided it was time to discuss with Ronald's parents the need for further assistance outside the classroom. She did so, suggesting that they meet with the school social worker, and she facilitated that contact.

On the occasions when teachers need to refer a student to other professional resources within the school system or the community, parents often feel uncomfortable, defensive, and guilty at the suggestion. Initially, they may reject or dispute the need and become angry at the advice. Sometimes parents feel they have failed or their child has failed them. It is helpful when the teacher does not react negatively to these parental responses. The teacher can facilitate the referral discussion by giving clear reasons for its necessity, showing emotional understanding of parental reactions, and offering different options for courses of action. Parents may talk with the school social worker, family physician or pediatrician, family minister, local mental health clinic, or a private child psychologist, psychiatrist, or counselor. Teachers help the referral process when they take the time to listen and provide reassurance and support. To prepare themselves for this process, teachers may find it helpful to discuss the experience of referral with someone on the school staff.

Making an Objective Review

There are times when children handle the stress events in their lives very well, sometimes surprisingly so. Others may not be so resourceful. The decision to intervene or to not intervene may be made at a point shortly following the stress event and the behavioral response. There may also be occasions following a decision not to intervene in which that decision may be reversed because an appropriate response is followed by an inappropriate response.

If a teacher is to incorporate successfully all the criteria described in the preceding discussion, practice is required. The more criteria that are considered in an intervention decision, the more appropriate the decision is likely to be. However, one should not be overly concerned if an intervention decision that is made on the spot does not include careful consideration of all these criteria. The teacher who is sensitive to the child in stress situations and makes well-intended attempts to assist that child to respond more positively is likely to be helpful and not harmful. Yet, it should be emphasized again that teachers' intuitive, confident feelings about what to do need the confirmation of objective criteria when possible.

9

Teacher Interventions

Teachers have long been empathic helpers of children, and children have turned to teachers for help with their problems at school and at home. In this sense, teachers are often therapeutic in their role with children, not as therapists but as helpers, confiders, suggesters, and supporters. Frequently, what teachers do and how they respond tend to be intuitively determined; that is, their responses are natural ones and are based upon insight and awareness of the child's feelings rather than rational thought. In this intuitive process, teachers sometimes refer to their own childhood experiences as members of families and former students in classrooms (Ross, 1965). They draw on these experiences in terms of the receiver (child) and the giver (parent and teacher), identifying with both. Most of the time this process goes on without conscious awareness, specific memory recall, or rational, objective thinking. There are moments when childhood memories become conscious, as in the examples given earlier in this book in which one teacher remembered his fears and phobia of snakes and another teacher recalled an episode of stealing when he was a boy. The capacity for being in touch with childhood events while maintaining an adult posture can be a helpful asset to a teacher in responding appropriately and sensitively to children in the classroom.

How Teachers Intervene

Teachers intervene with individual children and children in groups around issues of instruction and learning (Gage and Berliner, 1979), management (Kounin, 1970), and deviancy (Redl, 1959). In this book an additional issue for teachers is addressed; stress in the lives of children at school and home. Teachers who help with the identification and processing of stress in children not only facilitate the personality development of children but also reduce interference in academic learning and knowledge acquisition. Kounin (1970) and Redl (1959) recognize the intuitively determined responses of teachers to managerial and behavioral problems in the classroom, but they also advocate a rational, conceptual base for teacher responses to these issues. We are of similar persuasion in recommending an objective, rational, conceptual base for identifying, clarifying, appraising, intervening in, and monitoring stress and its processing in the classroom. Experiences with teachers and children suggest that a rational base for teacher interventions strengthens initial responses and provides a more powerful and effective impact on children's problems.

Teacher interventions aimed at dealing with stress in children are reactive in that they are initiated in response to or after a stressor has occurred and behavioral reactions have been identified. Reactive interventions are distinguished from proactive interventions, the latter being teacher responses initiated prior to or in anticipation of future stressful events or conditions. In chapter 14, the conceptual and applied aspects of proactive interventions are discussed in detail. It is important to recognize, however, that effective reactive interventions to current stressful events may have a proactive effect in that they may provide ways for a child to process future stressful events of a similar or different nature. Clinical experience suggests that successful stress resolution predicts successful adaptation to future stress (Moos & Billings, 1982).

Focus of Reactive Interventions

Where and how to intervene is part of the teacher appraisal process. Reactive interventions by teachers can focus on one or more aspects of the stress process, including the following:

1. *The stress event or situation.* Teachers can help to modify its characteristics, elements, and perceptions by a child.
2. *The behavioral reactions of the child.* Teachers can help to alter the nature and balance of feeling, thinking, action, and body responses (behavioral domains).
3. *The mediating variables of personal and environmental factors.*

These variables are found in the current and background status of the child and influence the nature of and response to stress events or situations. Teachers can help by mitigating unfavorable factors and accentuating positive ones.

4. *The behavioral processes of coping, defending, and fragmenting.* Teachers can provide assistance through suggesting, teaching, modeling, demonstrating, and advocating alternative and more effective process strategies.

The focus for intervention will depend on the feasibility, practicality, and potential impact of actions taken in each of these four areas.

Sometimes it is possible for a teacher to interrupt or change a chronic stress situation. In a stress situation in which a boy had been the repeated victim of a bully in the class, a teacher stopped the bullying episodes in and out of class directly and addressed the group attitudes and values of her class that permitted bullying. She involved both the bully and the whipping boy and their parents separately in problem-solving efforts with the school social worker to modify these respective behaviors (Olweus, 1978). Such interventions are focused directly on the stressor.

In another example, a child can be helped to view the single-parenthood status of his mother as acceptable, not uncommon, and preferable to having both parents together and quarreling. Even though different from many other families, this does not have to be seen as a source of shame. In this way, a child's perception of a stressful situation can be modified. The particular meaning attributed to a stress event by an individual can sometimes be clarified, as in those instances in which a child believes she or he is responsible for the event. The perception can be altered and the impact of the stress thereby reduced.

Teachers may focus their efforts on the behavioral reactions of a child. Feelings and physical actions of anger by a child against the teacher and classmates can be redirected into verbalization and cognitive expression. Thinking and verbalizing become alternative ways of reacting that may facilitate the processing of stress. An example is a child who complained and became angry at his teacher's unfairness and at the teasing by classmates. Through verbalizing feelings and thinking about reasons for feelings, he began to acknowledge his anger at his father for deserting the family and running off with another woman. After a while, this child stopped directing his anger at his teacher and classmates.

It may be possible for teachers to influence personal and environmental factors that may have mediating effects on stress. Some parents may be quite open, accessible, and responsive to suggestions from the teacher and other school personnel. For example, on his teacher's recommendation, one boy's parents were able to share with him their feelings and information about a proposed family move which resulted in more participation for the child. Such steps can affect environmental mediating factors in a favorable way and modify the child's negative perception of an event such as moving. Yet in another case, a family may not have sufficient time, energy, and resourcefulness to attend to the stressful reactions of their healthy child while dealing with the hospitalization and serious illness of another child with cystic fibrosis. A teacher may share in the crisis of such a family by providing support and attentiveness to the well child at school when the parents are not able to do so. Classmates can also be mobilized as supporters, helpers, and allies of the teacher in, for example, helping a student from Vietnam deal with unfamiliar, strange, and sometimes incomprehensible new life circumstannes.

The option of focusing interventions on the child's behavioral processes makes it possible to develop strategies that are more effective in dealing with stress. For example, a child may view a stress event largely in terms of anxiety and threat. An adult can appeal to the child to see the event as a challenge to be mastered and to demonstrate bravery and courage. Another child who is experiencing stress might be encouraged to recall upsetting life events in the past that had been handled positively.

In a specific example, a bright boy with chronic kidney disease seemed to feel less anxious and depressed when he could obtain a great deal of information about kidneys and kidney function. Greater cognitive understanding of an event of concern seemed to result in feelings of greater psychological control and predictability.

Categories of Reactive Interventions

Teachers' reactive interventions not only can be focused on different aspects of the stress process but also can be designed for different purposes and goals. These include cognitive understanding, emotional support, emotional expression, structure, control, and skill development. However, one reactive intervention may involve more than one purpose, such as channeling aggression, which provides emotional expression, structure, and control.

Because they reflect individual teacher differences and human variabilities, it would be very difficult to identify all possible reactive interventions. Even so, they can be organized into a smaller number of categories, depending upon their purposes. We obtained a large number of reactive interventions from a population of elementary school teachers who were applying the stress-intervention model in their classrooms. The teachers reported over seventy specific interventions, often used in various combinations. We have categorized these interventions, as presented in table 9.1, according to the following five purposes or intents:

1. Cognitive understanding
2. Emotional expression
3. Emotional support
4. Structure and control
5. Skill development

Some of the interventions can be categorized in more than one group. "Questioning," while listed under column 1, "cognitive understanding," also provides an opportunity for "emotional expression" (column 2), as indicated by the number "2" that has been placed after "questioning" in the first column of table 9.1. Similar numbers following other interventions in the table indicate that they also can be considered to be in more than one category.

The classification of reactive interventions into purpose categories provides a rational basis for selection. For example, if, according to the teacher's appraisal, a child needs to express feelings about a stressful event, then one or more of the interventions listed in the "emotional expression" column of table 9.1 may be appropriate. The specific interventions listed in their respective category columns should not be treated as a recipe of selections. Rather, the specific interventions suggest possible options and the categories indicate the purpose or goal of interventions. What is being suggested are guidelines for teachers rather than specific prescriptions or scripts to follow.

TABLE 9.1 *Specific Reactive Teacher Interventions, by Purpose Category*

(1) COGNITIVE UNDERSTANDING	(2) EMOTIONAL EXPRESSION	(3) EMOTIONAL SUPPORT	(4) STRUCTURE AND CONTROL	(5) SKILL DEVELOPMENT
Labeling feelings	Listening	Empathising	Providing structure	Recalling previous success
Clarifying	Permitting feelings	Acknowledging[1]	Helping organize	Modeling
Questioning[2]	Channeling agression[4]	Praising	Directing attention	Humor
Gathering information	Drawing	Physical contact	Modifying school expectations	Verbalizing [2] feelings
Explaining	Writing	Peer support-ing	Limit setting	Turning passive to active
Providing information	Role playing[5]	Showing concern	Isolating	Providing opportunity for choice
Exploring meanings	Talking in private	Reassuring	Firmness	Other perspectives
Interpreting	Reading books[1,4]	Sharing affect	Challenging[5]	Changing perspectives
Sharing truths[3]	Using films[3,4]	Involving parents	Time out	Problem and analysis[4]
Connecting event and feeling	Show and Tell	Giving attention	Reinforcing values	

Note: The number or numbers following an intervention refer to the other categories in which it could be included.

(continued)

TABLE 9.1 (*Continued*)

COGNITIVE UNDERSTANDING	EMOTIONAL EXPRESSION	EMOTIONAL SUPPORT	STRUCTURE AND CONTROL	SKILL DEVELOPMENT
Mirroring child responses		Showing concern	Advising	
		Encouraging	Realistic goals	
		One-to-one attention	Clear consequences	
		Comforting	Developing a plan	
		Advising parents	Maintaining personal perspective	
		Using personal experience	Putting problem aside	
		Feeding	Emphasizing positives[3]	
		Following up	Privacy to control	
		Class discussion	Confronting	
		Initally talking		
		Reducing guilt and shame		
		Being nonjudgmental		
		Acknowledging feelings		
		Offering help		

An example of a thoughtful and creative intervention is illustrated through Kim, an eleven-year-old girl in the fifth grade.

• While working on a reading assignment, Kim was asked by her teacher to reread a sentence that she had not read well. Kim gave a heavy sigh, her shoulders slumped and head dropped to her chest. She slapped her hand on the table and looked down at the book. Kim furrowed her eyebrows and began to reread in a disgusted, slow voice. On completing the sentence, Kim moved her chair back from the table and commented, "I can't ever get anything right." The teacher mirrored Kim's behaviors of sighing and slumping shoulders, whereupon Kim sighed and slumped again. Again the teacher copied her posture and nonverbal communications. This happened two more times, then Kim looked up and both she and the teacher smiled. The teacher felt that this initial intervention into a somewhat complex stressful life situation was effective. The teacher thought momentary relief of despair was helpful and humor was a way of reassuring Kim that it was acceptable to make mistakes. Further, the teacher was not angry, rejecting, or critical about the problem or about Kim. There was no judging or evaluation involved. The teacher respected the privacy of Kim's thoughts and feelings and did not feel comfortable about questioning Kim and encouraging her to talk at that time. She did later.

The teacher knew something about Kim's life situation. She was living with her aunt and uncle because her mother and stepfather moved around the country as migrant workers. Kim had attended four different schools in two different states over the last five years. The family had made no decision as to where Kim would be living in June when school was out. This would happen in about two months. The teacher inferred that Kim was anxious, depressed, and confused about her future, especially who would take care of her and where she preferred to live.

Her present and future living arrangements were the chronic stress situation in her life. The teacher's initial intervention focused on Kim's behavioral reactions of depression and poor school performance.

Assumptions Behind Reactive Interventions

The promotion of reactive interventions in the classroom is based on a number of assumptions. One of them is that such activities with children are within the teacher's accepted professional role. There is long-standing implicit permission for teachers to explore sensitive and private issues with children and to collaborate with their parents in fostering growth, competence, and positive adjustment. When this is done with tact, reasonableness, and sensitivity, it is very rare for difficulties to arise. If a teacher is uncomfortable and doubts the legitimacy of exercising this role, he or she needs to clear this up by talking with professional colleagues and administrators.

A second assumption is that teachers are viewed by students and most of their parents as being helping agents for children, beyond being facilitators of learning. As one thirteen-year-old girl stated, "If I had a problem, I'd go to my mother first, and if she couldn't help, I'd go to a teacher." (Kids need caring adults, 1984)

A third assumption is that a child has the right to personal privacy and to reject interventions on the part of the teacher, no matter how well meaning these may be. Respect needs to be given to the personal space of a child, and a child should be approached with that attitude.

Principles of Intervention

In addition to these assumptions, there are a number of principles in intervention. The teacher should have knowledge of practical interventions as well as skill in implementation. While advice and suggestions to teachers from sources outside the classroom are legitimate, unfortunately they are usually not available. In addition, teachers need to have sufficient emotional strength of their own, in order to deal with stress in children's lives. Teachers should not be expected to be therapists or superhumans. Also, it may be advisable for them to delay action in order to plan more judicious interventions. Teachers should not underestimate the potential power of their interventions with children, because they can be implemented five days a week by the same person and can be followed over an extended time period.

Other principles of intervention include recognizing that more than one specific intervention is usually employed and that one intervention often has multiple effects. However, it is important to persist with a few interventions, giving them a chance to be effective over time, rather than to change them frequently or increase their number. Increasing the numbers of interventions, much like increasing the dosage of medicine, may not strengthen potency but may create side-effects. In processing stress, a child needs to develop a balance between emotional expression and emotional control. Stress resolution and mastery are also fostered when a connection can be made between a stress event and the consequential behavioral reactions. Therefore both the event and behaviors need to be addressed.

Reappraisal

The processing of a stressful event and associated behaviors is not always achieved by a single reactive intervention applied at a certain time. Clinical experience indicates that the assimilation and resolution of stress takes time, depending on its severity, its consequences, the support systems available, and many other factors (Rutter, 1983). Teacher interventions may ease intensity or shorten the duration of the process, but not always. It is necessary to monitor the stress process to determine if the situation has worsened, remained the same, or improved. Reappraisal requires the same judgments as discussed previously in initial appraisal: intensity of the stressor, appropriateness of response, duration of the process, pervasiveness, and unusualness of response. Based on reappraisal, a decision may be made to continue, discontinue, or revise interventions. In some situations where no progress has been made, referral of the child to other school and community resources should be considered.

Keri, a nine-year-old girl, provides an example of teacher interventions applied over a period of a week that resulted in the reestablishment of adaptive behavior.

• Keri was usually an excellent student with an outgoing personality. She had many friends and was the center of social action in the classroom. She thought and felt sensitively about happenings in her world. Keri came from a stable, close, and intact family. Recently she was told by her parents that her father was going to another state for a job interview. Her teacher discovered this stress event when Keri came to her one morning and said, "Mrs. Sears, we might move." Over the next several days Keri had a worried and tense look on her face, teared easily, lacked her usual concentration on schoolwork, and failed to follow directions several times because she was preoccupied with her thoughts. The teacher was tempted to reassure Keri that the move would work out all right, but instead found time to talk with her in private, acknowledge feelings, label emotions, and give permission to feel. Mrs. Sears acknowledged that it was sad to leave friends, labeled moving as a hard thing for Keri to get out of her mind, and gave permission to feel by crying about loneliness. A week later Keri told her teacher that she wasn't thinking about moving as much as she used to.

Summary

Reactive interventions can be focused on one or more of four aspects of the stress process:

1. The stress event or situation
2. Behavioral reactions
3. Mediating variables from the current status and background of the child, reflecting psychological disequilibrium
4. Behavioral processes of coping, defending, and fragmenting

Interventions can be directed at the child experiencing stress, the family, and the various environmental influences at home and school.

The specific nature of reactive interventions by teachers can be categorized according to purpose, intent, and goal. Five different purposes can be identified:

1. Cognitive understanding
2. Emotional expression
3. Emotional support
4. Structure and control
5. Skill development

In practice teachers will use a number of specific interventions, some of them having multiple purposes.

Processing and resolving stress in children involves allowing time to experience, assimilate, and adapt to the nature of the event and associated behaviors. Therefore, a teacher follows the progress of the child through a monitoring procedure, also called reappraisal. Reappraisal determines whether interventions should be continued, discontinued, or revised.

10

Family-Related Stressors

Coddington's (1972) "Life Events Questionnaire" and Garmezy's (1981) stress inventory, described briefly in chapter 1, make clear that certain life events to which children are subject are common stressors of varying potential impact. Efforts to quantify the intensity of the stressors are of dubious usefulness because of the influences of the many mediating variables that have been described throughout this book. Yet the identification of stressors and the estimates of their relative impact by independent investigators are helpful in focusing attention on the range of conditions that may induce stress in children.

In this and the following two chapters, examples of the possible effects of common stressors are elaborated. Readers who have worked with children are likely to recognize episodes from their own experience that may have paralleled these vignettes or may have resulted in quite different consequences.

Stressors chosen for illustration are believed to occur frequently, to have a noticeable impact on children, to link with other high-impact stressors, and to be related to school performance. Some of the events have their origin in family structure, while others result from extreme behaviors of parents, from personal or family health problems, and from school happenings. Suggestions for teacher interventions are mentioned only implicitly.

In this chapter, common family-related stressors will be presented.

Divorce

For children, according to Wallerstein and Kelly (1980a, b), the traumatic potential of divorce is second only to the death of a parent. A child experiences a sense both of loss and of vulnerability to forces beyond his or her control. Fears, sadness, and anger are mobilized. Approximately one million children each year witness the breakup of their families by separation and divorce (Children's Defense Fund, 1979).

For five-year-old Julie and her eight-year-old brother Dan, the divorce their parents were going through was a series of crises. Julie and Dan span the age range at which children may be most vulnerable, and certainly it is the one in which the largest number of children are affected.

- At five Julie was old enough to know that her parents were not getting along well and that they were in the process of ending their marriage. Quite typical of her age and sex, Julie's major fears were of abandonment and deprivation. She was sad and tormented by vague thoughts that she might have somehow caused her parents to separate. Though she wished her mother and father would come back together, she was persuaded that they would not. Her behavioral reactions were to withdraw into her grief, giving expression to it by crying, whining, and displaying dependent behavior atypical for her age.

  Dan shared Julie's feelings of fearfulness and possible responsibility for disrupting his parents' marriage. He was inclined to assume responsibilities for the care of the family that went beyond his developmental age level. He tried to replace his missing father, with whom he was angry. This was expressed through irrational behaviors such as attempting to stay awake all night to protect his mother and sister from imagined burglars. At school Dan exhibited aggressive, bullying behaviors quite unlike his earlier demeanor.

  In some ways the household had become quieter, since the arguing and emotional outbursts of mother and father were no longer heard. But there were mixed loyalties, loneliness, and anger—at being separated from the father and at the mother who was less available because of her extended responsibilities for the house and family.

The fear of abandonment, the anger, and the sense of responsibility for their parents' difficulties are typical reactions of elementary schoolchildren experiencing the stress of parental divorce. However, a variety of mediating factors influence the effects of divorce on children, in individual ways. The impact of divorce should be viewed in that way. The open display of rancor between the parents, the care with which the parents assure and reassure the children of their continued love and concern for them, the steps taken to limit the disruption of the children's lives, and the sharing of reasons why the parents feel compelled to separate are a few of the important variables that may reduce the impact of divorce on children.

Thoughtful parents can do much to relieve children of the burdens of divorce. In a similar way, teachers can do much for children to alleviate the stressfulness of disharmony in the home. The child who can stay in the same school and maintain peer and teacher relationships through a period of turmoil in the home is apt to feel more support than the child who must move. For the child who is uprooted from home and school, the transition can be eased by sensitive teachers at each end of the transition. The teacher who is being left can acknowledge the child's uncertainties and reduce the fantasized fears by speaking openly of the realities of changing schools. A letter of introduction to the receiving teacher, along with an adequately documented record of academic achievement, will do much to prepare a place for the child in the classroom of the receiving teacher. A well-informed receiving teacher can acknowledge the child's presence among the new classmates as well as show private understanding of the circumstances that have caused the child to change schools.

Recognition that divorce is stressful for children, even under the best of circumstances, is basic to understanding the children who are experiencing or have experienced this stressor. School achievement may lag, interpersonal relationships may shift, emotional outbursts may occur, dependencies may emerge, and age-related behaviors may give way to immaturities. The teacher can provide an appropriate blend of tolerance and expectation as means to understanding the situation and respecting the child's ability to rise above adversity.

The One-Parent Family

It is estimated that close to one-half of today's children will spend part of their childhood with just one parent, usually the mother (Keniston, 1977). In 1981, 19 percent of U.S. children lived with one parent, representing 6.6 million families (Sanoff, 1982). One metropolitan school district in Michigan reported a mean mobility rate of children among its elementary schools of 33.7 percent, but the mobility rate of children from one-parent homes was 44.2 percent (Blom,

1980b). It is very clear that family forms in this country are changing, and it is doubtful that schools have adjusted to the new reality of the one-parent family.

A report written for the National Committee for Citizens in Education (Collins, 1981) indicates that of 1,200 single parents in forty-seven states who were surveyed, 39 percent were dissatisfied with the treatment that they and their children received from schools. The use of the "broken home" descriptor by school personnel (a pejorative reference), social events such as "Breakfast with Dad," and the making of gifts in school for parents not living in the child's home were noted in this study as examples of schools' failures to recognize changed family structures. The frequent assumption, either implied or expressed, that any school problems the children of single parents have are somehow related to family form was resented by the questionnaire respondents. Single-parents also reported their concern about schoolbooks that continue to depict only two-parent homes as being normal. Among the schools surveyed, only about one in twenty informed noncustodial parents about school activities or sent them progress reports on their children, yet these rights are secured for all parents by the Federal Family Educational Rights and Privacy Act of 1974.

Clearly, it is both insensitive and invalid for school professionals to stereotype negatively the millions of children and adults who live in one-parent families. The vast majority of these homes provide an environment that is adequately supportive and challenging for child rearing. There can, of course, be differences between homes with two parents and homes with one. One-parent homes may offer less financial security, peer relationships may have more significance to children, children may be required to accept more family responsibilities, and children may experience more loyalty conflicts between their parents. As with other types of diversity, differences in family form should be accepted and responded to at the individual level by schools. This means that not all children of one-parent families need a replacement for the absent parent and that not every child with one parent goes home to an empty house. There is stress in all families, and one-parent families are not exceptions.

The range of variables that distinguishes one-parent families from each other is probably as extensive as the range among two-parent families. The cause of singleness is one of these variables. Parents may be single as a result of never having married, divorce, death of a spouse, criminal incarceration, prolonged hospitalization, occupational demands, and many other reasons. It is evident that any of these circumstances might have a profound and complex influence upon the lives of family members. It is equally clear that the identification of any particular circumstance may reveal other related variables that may interact in quite unpredictable ways. The point is that any consideration of the solitary impact of the single-parent family on the behaviors of children is oversimplified. The meaning of single parenthood as a potential stressor in the life of a child can only be assessed in the context of all the related variables that pertain in an individual case (Ogg, 1976).

Children of single parents are sometimes observed to behave as if they are older than other children their age. One explanation for this is the rather common role they play as confidants for their parents, who may be without regular access to listening adults. Participation in these adultlike conversations may cause them to acquire adult concerns and interests, possibly reducing some of the playfulness of childhood. Some child advocates, including Elkind (1982), are alarmed by this "parentification of the child." An alternative view is to see parentification as possibly challenging and as a source of gratification for the child.

There are good reasons for believing that single parents are subjected to greater stress than are parents who can share family duties and responsibilities. Incomes often are more limited, household duties are not shared, adult companionship is less accessible, and discretionary time is less available for the single parent. Under these conditions, it takes a strong person to satisfy personal and family needs, yet single parents commonly meet the challenges of their situations.

Just as parents are urged to consider their children's needs during and after the period of their separation, schools also should adjust their practices. Some of these adjustments are matters of awareness and sensitivity that cost nothing; most of the other adjustments cost very little. Small but important adjustments relate to the scheduling of parent conferences, awareness and attention to the legal rights of both parents, recognition of the variety of family forms in class discussions, and general sensitivity to the needs of children who may be feeling a personal loss or who may need to divide their time between two homes. More complex adjustments involve the selection of texts and other books that depict the one-parent family as well as other family forms and the development of after-school programs that accommodate some of the child-care needs of single-parent families.

Latchkey Children

Due to the image of the house key they may wear around their necks or pinned to their clothing, a sizable number of children who go home to empty houses have been dubbed "latchkey" children. These are some of the children of working parents, children who are considered mature enough by their parents and usually by themselves not to need a babysitter or daycare. Frequently latchkey children are responsible for the care of brothers and sisters as well as for themselves, thus adding to the adult expectation that childhood should resemble adulthood in important ways.

Acknowledgment of the existence of latchkey children need not be tantamount to condemning the parents and the society that spawned them, but in cases of poor parental judgment there is reason to do so. Immature children who are alone, isolated, and ill prepared to care for themselves are exposed to physical as well as psychological dangers. The school, as an institution with teachers and principals as its agents, bears a responsibility to at least monitor and question instances when more self-sufficiency is expected of children than is reasonable. It is desirable for the school to take a far more proactive role, by offering after-school programs for latchkey children and promoting parental awareness of the need for social and emotional nurturance.

Let's consider the following case example.

• Eleven-year-old Jack, son of educated and professionally employed parents, seemed mature beyond his years. If any child was competent enough to carry a house key and open the home for the family each afternoon, Jack was. Jack had looked forward to being a fifth grader because it meant that he would no longer need to go to the home of a babysitter after school. After all, what eleven year old can easily accept the notion that he or she must be supervised by a babysitter?

Jack lived in a nice home in a suburban neighborhood populated by successful people. He could walk a few blocks with friends from school to his home. The routine was well established: No friends were to come into the house with him. He was to change his clothes, get a snack for himself, and do something "constructive" until his parents arrived home at about 5:15. "Constructive" was understood to mean work on his models, read library books selected with the interested participation of his parents, or play with children outside in his own yard or in the nearby yard of one of his friends. Anything that took him away from home required a note of explanation left for his parents and a return to the home no later than 5:30. He knew better than to ride with strangers, and he was to enter the homes of friends known to his parents only if parents were in the home at the time. All the precautions had been taken. Jack was a good student, a wholesome boy, relatively free of fears. His friends were very acceptable to his parents. He was instructed in how to use emergency telephone numbers and his parents' work numbers. The plan was working beautifully. His parents noticed that Jack was becoming more self-assured and competent as the weeks went on.

After a while, however, wet, cold, dark days of November reduced the inclination of the neighborhood boys to play outside, requiring that they isolate themselves indoors more of the time. One of the boys, Eric, developed a new line of conversation as the children walked together to and from school: Eric's investigation of his parents' liquor cabinet. As a matter of curiosity Eric began to sample a few of the open bottles. He spoke of his dislike of many of the flavors, but he persisted in sampling others out of curiosity. He was aware that his parents consumed alcohol in moderation and that to do otherwise would result in drunkenness or out-of-control behavior. Not wishing to be discovered in his new activity, he was careful to sip very little of any bottles sampled and to restrict the sampling range to only a couple of bottles. Beer and wine were problems, however, because those bottles were not open and to sample them would reveal his subterfuge. For a week or more, each new day's conversation described the samplings of the afternoon before, with Eric's audience eager to listen.

Group problem solving was at its best when the boys were trying to come up with an undetectable procedure for sampling beer and wine. It did not take long for them to agree that the best approach would be to remove one bottle of beer or wine from the storage area at a time when there were enough bottles present to make the absence of one inconspicuous. Not long after the plan was set, Eric invited his friends to step into the garage to have a taste of the wine while hiding behind some seldom-used firewood. All agreed that the stuff did not taste very good but the activity was very exciting. Eric even found himself in a situation with some power and control in that it was he who could determine the participants in the afternoon wine-tasting party. Since the wine bottles were large, the afternoon stop-off at Eric's garage became quite routine, an activity looked forward to by the group of aspiring adults. Even the taste of the stuff improved. Other liquor cabinets in the neighborhood were investigated, even Jack's.

It was just a matter of time until the daily gathering at Eric's was noticed by a neighbor and the whistle was blown. Inventive stories were offered to inquiring parents. Parental reactions ranged from understanding to irrational anger. Since the boys' feelings of curiosity and excitement had evolved to feelings of guilt, their reactions upon being caught ranged from relief at having been absolved of sin to righteous anger for having been yelled at for doing what parents do as a matter of right.

The reaction of Eric's parents promoted a defensive posture in Eric that developed into a continuous challenge of their authority to curtail his behavior. Jack was more fortunate. Although his parents were annoyed, they understood the misdemeanor as experimental behavior that can be expected in the circumstances in which children live; and they also felt a bit of remorse for not having initiated conversations about drinking and the uses of alcohol earlier. The incident was a turning point for Jack and his parents in opening their relationship to discussions of new issues of importance to young people moving toward adulthood. Jack's good fortune with his parents led to greater trustworthiness on his part and the continuation of his independence as a latchkey child. For Eric and some of the others it was the end of self-sufficiency and a return to a dependency status for some time that was itself demeaning to the children.

What could the school have done in this situation? Certainly teachers and principals cannot assume responsibility for intelligent parenting. They can, however, anticipate the hazards of growing up in our society and work cooperatively with parents, to prepare them for occurrences that are virtually inevitable. There is a predictability about experimentation with alcohol and other drugs that warrants educational efforts by school staffs in smoothing the way for children in these risk areas (Finn & O'Gorman, 1981). The concept of childcare that assigns responsibility for social and emotional development to parents and cognitive development to schools fails to deal with the realities of childhood and responsible concern for the welfare and socialization of children.

Adding a Stepparent to the Family

Children of the single-parent family frequently undergo another event of potential stressfulness: the addition of a stepparent to the family. This is not an infrequent event since today four out of five divorced parents eventually remarry; the average time between divorce and remarriage is three years (Keniston, 1977). Under ideal circumstances the addition of the new parent is an occasion for joy and the beginning of an improved quality of life for the child. The child who has been included in activities during the period of courtship, who has had the opportunity to get acquainted with the adult friend, and who does not fear the loss of love or status in the eyes of the continuing parent should have less trouble adjusting to the new authority figure in the family.

Even when caring adults make efforts to ease the transition for the children, there may be other variables that interfere with the acceptance of a stepparent. Children with active affection and association with the natural parent who has been absent from the household may resent the intrusion of another parent who becomes the object of attention in the home. Stepparents who do not possess the qualities of the absent but well-loved natural parent may have a hard time winning respect from the skeptical or fearful child. Access to the absent parent may be curtailed by the presence of the stepparent. New standards of conduct in the home may cause resentment or even rebelliousness. With adults who are newly in love and in the process of adjusting to each other in important ways, the child may feel left out and anxious. Children who have become accustomed to adultlike conversations with one parent and who enjoyed the role of confidant and heightened responsibility may feel slighted or downgraded by the new parent who assumes this niche in the family (Group for the Advancement of Psychiatry, 1973).

Stepparents who bring their own families into homes where children already reside compound the impact of a new family structure. The parents have chosen each other and are in love, but usually the children of the two parents have had little association or opportunity to express feelings about each other. The ages, sexes, numbers, interests, abilities, habits, expectations, personality traits, and other personal attributes of children of the merged families will affect them all. If private space must suddenly be shared, if cherished possessions become cooperatively owned, if parent time and attention must now be shared, if home life becomes competitive, if rules of acceptable behavior must be merged, it is little wonder that behavioral indicators of stress may surface. Having a new playmate is a wonderful thing; sharing one's life with the new playmate is possibly less wondrous.

Death of a Family Member

About 9 percent of children in this country will lose one or both parents to death before they reach the age of eighteen (Bane, 1976). It is therefore highly desirable that teachers be prepared to deal with children who are grieving for a lost parent. This is illustrated in the following case example.

• Mrs. Gilmore read in the local paper that Mark's father had died while shoveling snow during the school's midwinter vacation. She had immediately sent a card to the family and a brief note to seven-year-old Mark. She dreaded returning to school to confront Mark because she anticipated that the trauma of his father's death would have a profound impact on him. In trying to think through an appropriate approach, Mrs. Gilmore recalled that Mark's sister was seventeen, his mother worked outside the home, and his father had seemed like an affable man on the one occasion when he had come to school for a parent conference. Mark spoke fondly of the experiences he and his father had shared. She was convinced that the child's loss would be agonizing and bewildering. She wished she knew more specifically how Mark was reacting. She felt unprepared by previous training or experience to deal with a child in grief.

On Monday following the vacation Mrs. Gilmore was relieved to find that Mark was not at school. This would give her time to prepare the other children for Mark's return to the classroom. As they arrived, a few of the children revealed that they too knew about the death of Mark's father; for many others it came as news, mostly acquired in talking to their classmates as they waited near the door to enter the school. The children varied widely in their reactions. Some appeared to be genuinely saddened, some were excited about an event of such magnitude, others were concerned about Mark, and a few were unusually quiet, seemingly perplexed.

After quieting the children and greeting them, Mrs. Gilmore acknowledged the death of Mark's father, sharing some of her own concerns about the impact of such an event upon Mark and his family. Children who wished to ask questions, express their own feelings, or share personal experiences related to death of a loved one were allowed to do so.

After a few minutes of spontaneous discussion, Mrs. Gilmore asked the children to consider how they would feel in Mark's place and how they would wish to be treated when they returned to school. Many suggestions were offered, with some receiving spoken and unspoken assent and dissent from classmates. The general tone of this discussion, as reflected to the children by Mrs. Gilmore, was to support those remarks that suggested acknowledgment of Mark's loss, expression of caring for Mark and his family, and acceptance of any changes in Mark's behavior. The expectation that "business as usual" in the classroom would be a way of providing Mark a dependable and reassuring environment was suggested to the children and accepted by them. It was also agreed that the afternoon art project would be to create colorful cards with reassuring messages to place on Mark's desk.

While the children were at recess, Mrs. Gilmore called Mark's home to speak with his mother. After expressing her condolences she inquired about Mark's reaction to his father's death and about the plans for returning to school. She learned that the family had gone to the maternal grandparents' home following the funeral to spend a few days in a different environment. While there, Mark and his mother, sister, and grandparents talked about his father's death and what his absence would mean in their lives. Mark observed his mother's grief and was allowed to express his own, and his grandfather encouraged Mark to become involved in normal family activities. Mark experienced a variety of emotions, including sadness, fear, self-pity, anger, and even tranquility as more intense emotional reactions were relieved by self-expression and the acceptance of adult members of the family.

Mrs. Gilmore was relieved to hear about the ways in which the family had reacted to the death. Mark's family respected his needs to express grief and to adjust to profound loss. The discussion with Mark's mother helped Mrs. Gilmore to confirm a plan to provide a normal classroom climate, allowing for open expression of feelings and curiosity among the children, with emotional support and acceptance from her. To help Mark's classmates understand the impact of the loss of a parent, she introduced and read aloud a book about a girl who has trouble coming to terms with the reality of the death of her mother. When Mark returned to the class, she planned to interrupt reading the book aloud until she could determine when he was ready to participate with the other children in discussing the book.

Problem Drinking in the Family

The drinking behavior of Americans ranges from total abstinence to alcoholism, or extreme alcohol dependence. Schoolchildren come from homes in which this wide range of practice pertains. Whatever the drinking practices of the family are, it is reasonable to assume that they have an effect on the children. The abstinent family, for example, may have an extreme and forbidding parental posture toward drinking that tends to further incite the curiosity or experimental and rebellious behaviors of children. Abstinent families may reject alcohol consumption on religious or moral grounds, on grounds of maintaining health, out of fear that the first drink opens the door for eventual alcoholism, or for many other reasons. Even though not drinking is a valid choice, in our drinking society the abstinence position is a difficult one to maintain because children cannot be sheltered successfully from drinking behavior. The ubiquitous home television is but one obvious source of information about drinking that is readily accessible to children.

Family alcoholism is on the opposite end of the continuum of drinking behaviors to which children are exposed. The effect on children of alcoholism in the family is mediated by such intervening variables as the child's age, the extent of exposure to the problem drinker, the child's perception of family stability, whether there is disharmony between the parents, whether it is the father or mother who drinks, and many others. The stressor of problem drinking and the various mediating variables combine in unpredictable ways to influence the child (Blom, Cheney, & Snoddy, 1982).

Two cautions about alcoholism and the children of alcoholics are important. Current conventional wisdom tends to accept alcoholism as a disease and the children of alcoholics to be at risk for that disease. These two conceptions should be examined further in terms of their implications for treatment and prevention.

The disease conception of alcoholism got its start in the early 1930s, coincident with the rise of Alcoholics Anonymous and the establishment of clinics for the treatment of alcoholics (Howland & Howland, 1978). Advocates of the disease concept see alcoholism in its symptomatic form as chemical dependency that requires medical, psychological, and social treatment. Some alcohologists see alcoholism as the final result of an innate biological predisposition combined with alcohol consumption. The person afflicted with alcoholism is believed to have been predisposed or vulnerable as a consequence of an allergy, genetic transmission, or atypical tissue response. The disease concept may relieve the alcoholic of personal responsibility for the condition, as is the case with infections or other types of illness. There is also, in this view, no cure for alcoholism, only a remission that is gained through complete abstention, as proposed by Alcoholics Anonymous. Some controversy now exists over the possibility that a recovering alcoholic might resume social drinking in moderation and gain control without reverting to illness, but the predominant view remains that alcoholism, once established, is only controlled by not drinking at all (Armor, Polich, & Braiker, 1980).

Disproportionately high numbers of children of alcoholics wind up becoming alcoholics themselves. Because of this, they are said to be at risk for alcoholism. School programs describing the range of drinking/nondrinking behaviors are particularly appropriate for these vulnerable children (Finn & O'Gorman, 1981). It is important to note, however, that over half of the children of alcoholic parents do not succumb to alcoholism, either as youths or adults.

Elementary schoolchildren know some things about alcohol and drinking behavior (Jahoda & Cramond, 1972). In an unpublished study of ours, we interviewed first-, third-, and fifth-grade children to determine their knowledge and attitudes about drinking and non-drinking. The children were from one-parent and two-parent, non-abstaining families living in a variety of neighborhoods in and around Lansing, Michigan.

It was found that children

1. Are aware of alcoholic beverages and have developed knowledge and feelings about drinking by the time they start school
2. Know and accept that alcohol is approved for adults but forbidden to them
3. Express no particular desire to drink but look forward to a wider choice of adult activities, especially driving, attending parties, and using various tools and appliances
4. Want to know why people drink and what it feels like to be drunk
5. Tend to equate drinking with drunkenness and view it as a dangerous thing requiring adult maturity

6. Are uncomfortable around adults who are drinking, possibly because of their uncertainties about the effects of alcohol
7. Are aware that a lot of drinking is done on television but do not infer from the programs why adults drink
8. Do not hear much from adults about why they drink or how they feel when they do so

Children living with problem drinkers who are subjected to or witness physical or psychological abuse that would seem intolerable often remain loyal and affectionate toward their drinking parent. Tommy, a kindergartner, was such a child.

• Tommy's alcoholic father verbally and physically abused him, his third-grade sister, and his mother. In a particularly dramatic episode the mother ran from the home with the children, to escape the father's violence. Even after the father was placed in jail, she was fearful that he would be released, so she stayed with friends for several days.

Tommy was usually pleasant when talking with an adult, but he was a behavior problem at school, fighting and ridiculing his playmates frequently. When struck by his father at home, he defied him by refusing to cry, yet at school he expressed pride in his father. When not drunk his father could be warm and friendly with members of the family, and Tommy collected toy tools in order to become a mechanic like his father when he grew up.

Tommy's loyalty to his father, who was abusive when drinking, is not unlike that of many other children in similar circumstances. Tommy displayed some strengths for his age, but his school behaviors indicated a child in stress. Problem drinking in the family is a chronic stressor that places Tommy in an at-risk situation that may have long-term effects on him in child and adult life. It is not possible to predict what these effects will be. He may learn to cope with his stressful situation and may even gain strength in doing so. More likely, he will learn strategies for defending himself against the stressors he lives with. More negatively, he may succumb to the stressors that afflict him and may continue to display acting out behaviors; in adult life Tommy may identify with his father by drinking like him. The influence of a teacher may provide the emotional support and cognitive skills to avoid the long-term negative effects of this chronic stress.

Child Abuse and Neglect

"Since the beginning of time, the world's children have consti-
tuted an endangered species: a yielding target for the frustrations,
conflicts, projections, unresolved hates, and smoldering anger of the
adults who so often tyrannically bestride their lives" (Segal & Yahraes, 1978, p. 171). This statement expresses the indignation that most
people feel toward child abuse, an experience that has afflicted children and demeaned adults throughout history. Some 20 years ago,
child abuse was finally given visible identification (Kempe, 1962), but
the world of 1985 is not much more enlightened, in practice, than the
one of 1962. It is a rare teacher who does not know abused or neglected children.

The range of abuse that some children suffer at the hands of their
parents or other adult caregivers is shocking. This is illustrated by one
extreme example reported by the National Committee for the Prevention of Child Abuse (1982): A father, apparently imbued with an
image of male toughness, commonly spoke of his son as a "sissy" and,
on at least one occasion, forced the boy's hand into boiling water in
a misguided effort to toughen him. When the child screamed out of
pain, the father slapped his face to eliminate the expression of weak-
ness. There is no indication that this boy died as a result of abuse,
though he surely could have if such mistreatment continued. It is estimated that somewhere between .5 million and 1.5 million cases of
child abuse occur annually. Most do not result in death, but 1,000 to
3,000 of these cases are estimated to be fatal (Starr, 1979).

Burns, bruises, and broken bones are only the most evident indicators of child abuse; evidence is accumulating to link various behavioral consequences of child abuse and neglect as well. Abused children
often suffer from low intellectual functioning, social withdrawal, ap-
athy, aggressive behavior, physical disabilities, and poor health status (Helfer & Kempe, 1976). Dwarfism has been described as
resulting directly from severe child abuse (Money, 1977). In such
cases, the child, existing in conditions of extreme abuse, simply stops
growing physically and mentally. In cases where the dwarfed children have been removed from the abusive home environments, they
have resumed natural growth and have improved their intelligence
quotients and school achievement.

The 1974 Michigan Child Abuse and Neglect Act defines abuse and neglect as "the physical or mental injury, sexual abuse, negligent treatment or maltreatment of a child under age eighteen by a person who is responsible for the child's welfare" (Michigan, 1974, p. 2). Child abuse and neglect are present at all socioeconomic levels, but there is a higher incidence of it in families of low socioeconomic levels. It may be considered an expression of family stress, occurring frequently in socially isolated families in which the parents themselves were abused or neglected as children. Problem drinking or alcoholism is a factor in perhaps as many as one-third of child abuse cases.

Adults known to be child abusers have been described as having low tolerance for frustration, low self-esteem, high degrees of impulsivity and dependency, moods of severe depression, difficulty in experiencing pleasure, little understanding of the needs of children, and an almost childlike preoccupation with self. Studies listing personality traits of child abusers have failed to construct a consistent, generalized portrait of the child abuser; however, abusive parents have been consistently described as accepting abuse as a way of parental life, holding unrealistic expectations for children, frequently viewing child behaviors as evil, and having a history of abuse or neglect in their own childhoods. The next generation of abusive parents will come mainly from the present population of abused children (Helfer & Kempe, 1976).

State legislation has fostered the notion that it is the social responsibility of every citizen to report suspected cases of child abuse to local or state authorities who have responsibility for child protection. In some states, teachers and other professionals who deal directly with children are required by law to report suspected cases of child abuse. Such laws place a high value on the rights of children, to the extent of providing immunity from prosecution for adults who report suspected cases of abuse, even if they turn out to be in error (Erickson, McEvoy, & Colucci, 1979).

The recognition of cases of child abuse or neglect is a matter of judgment, requiring for a final determination a complete investigation of the circumstances present in the home, by officers legally responsible for child protection. Teachers and other caregivers seldom have all the facts at their disposal, but this should not deter them from reporting their own well-founded suspicions of abuse or neglect. Examples of situations that might constitute child abuse or neglect include those in which children are

1. Beaten or show other indications of cruel treatment
2. Abandoned by their caretaker
3. Poorly clothed, ill-fed, or dirty
4. Ill, with no medical attention provided
5. Overworked or exploited
6. Unsupervised or unattended much of the time, especially at night
7. Kept home from school for reasons other than illness
8. Sexually abused or molested
9. Not provided adequate shelter or sanitation (Michigan, 1974)

Interventions for child abuse and neglect can include child foster care, Parents Anonymous, self-help groups, nurseries, and short-term residential treatment. Most families receive multiple services. Increased efforts need to be made in prevention, including screening measures, visits by home health workers, education for parenthood, and, in our view, elimination of corporal punishment in schools.

Many schools and school districts have developed procedures for helping teachers in the reporting process, so that they do not stand alone and so that others can share responsibility in the decision. For example, one school district in Michigan has a two-person reporting team—a social worker and nurse. Another district makes use of the attendance officer in reporting. In many school districts, however, if teachers are to substantially increase their effectiveness in reporting instances of child abuse and neglect, then school boards and administrators will need to take more informed and active roles. School boards need to adopt policies that acknowledge the schools' responsibilities in abuse and neglect. Administrators at all levels must be more aware of these responsibilities and of the resources available in their own communities to assist in abuse and neglect cases. They need to implement reporting and referral systems in their communities.

This stark reality needs to be tempered by the recognition that poor living conditions may not always be indicative of child abuse or neglect. One child was described by a teacher as living in an urban home without adequate heat and expressing joy at the prospect of moving into the home of friends during the cold months because the friends had running water. He lived with his mother and sister, sharing in the misfortunes and limited joys of the family. This particular boy seemed to excel at school, despite the physical deprivation at home, and showed adaptive capacities and maturity beyond his age. His concern for his mother and sister, his strength in the face of adversity, and his acceptance of hardship without self-pity placed him among a small group of children who are sometimes described as invulnerable to the environmental crises that they face. Difficult as his living conditions were, he was not physically or emotionally abused, nor did he perceive himself as being neglected. Nonetheless, we do not advocate condoning societal neglect of poor living conditions for children or adults.

Summary

Family-related stressors of divorce, one-parent status, unsupervised children, stepparenthood, death in the family, problem drinking, and child abuse and neglect are usually known to teachers and school personnel. Their impact varies from one individual child or family to another. Frequently, they result in stress, which will usually be reflected in behaviors at school. While there is a danger that a teacher may develop negative expectations of children exposed to family stressors, the teacher can often provide helpful emotional and cognitive interventions to children experiencing stress. The first step for the teacher is to be aware of and willing to acknowledge what may be present in the family life situation of a child.

11

Health-Related Stressors

Teachers often lack information about health and illness topics. It is here that school nurses can be invaluable resources about the medical status of individual children and sources of medical information in general. It is always a good idea to consider the health status of a child in relation to a change in behavior, because, as parents well know, behaviors such as irritability, loss of energy, sadness, and vague somatic distress may be the first indicators of illness. However, there are many ways in which stressful life events are related to illnesses and their treatment and consequences.

Psychosomatic Disorders

Psychosomatic disorders are physical illnesses that are brought on by a specific biological predisposition for an individual to respond to physical, social, and psychological factors by becoming ill. Situational life events are often associated with the onset and recurrence of disease and with its refractoriness to medical treatment (Bemporad & Wuhl, 1978). These disorders in childhood include asthma, eczema, dermatitis, peptic ulcer, ulcerative colitis, and rheumatoid arthritis.

In asthma, which has a prevalence of 2 percent in children, a hyperactive respiratory tract exists as a consitutional biological response. This response can be triggered by respiratory illness, atmospheric or dietary allergens, climate changes, and acute or chronic situational stress. These triggers may act singly or additively and vary in importance and intensity from episode to episode of asthma. Furthermore, the consequences of asthma become additional stressors, including the frightening experience of asthmatic attacks, school absences, hospitalizations, dietary and exercise restrictions at home and school, desensitization injections, and understandable parental concerns and overprotectiveness. It is important to know that medications for treating asthma have caused behavioral side-effects of psychological origin. Stressful situational events that have been reported to trigger asthmatic attacks include birth of a sibling, parental illness, starting school initially or after vacation breaks, and marital discord (Blom, 1971). These stressors produce nonspecific disequilibrium effects but do not represent specific categories of events, as was previously thought.

Let's consider an example.

• Teresa, age ten, and her brother, Victor, age eight, had been in the same POHI (physically ill and otherwise health impaired) program because of Teresa's allergies and bouts of severe hives and Victor's allergies and episodes of asthma. Attempts were being made to provide some regular mainstream educational experiences for these children in separate classes. Both parents were anxious and demanding, and mistrustful and critical of teachers, principal, and lunch program staff, and almost every decision that was made by the school. The children were the only ones to bring allergen-free sack lunches to school every day. They had many school absences because of illnesses, they were fearful of separating from each other, and they had concerns about the children in the regular education class. The teacher consultant was able to encourage the school staff to be patient and not be provoked by the behaviors of the parents and the manipulativeness of the children. Finally, the parents told the consultant that they had both had surgical operations for cancer during the last five years. He felt that their anxieties about their own welfare were being transmitted to the children but that dealing with this issue should be the responsibility of a private psychiatrist. With much encouragement from the school, the parents made favorable contact with a psychiatrist; together, she and the school staff were able to make slow gains in reducing anxiety and making transitions to regular and more normalized school activities.

Chronic Illness

There are also chronic illnesses and physical disorders in which the course, treatment, recovery, and rehabilitation of an illness can be influenced by stressful life events (Whitt, 1984). These disorders and disabilities include diabetes (affects .16 percent of the child population less than eighteen years of age), seizures (affect .25 percent of the child population), sickle-cell disease, cystic fibrosis, hemophilia, burns, and other chronic illnesses (Kempe, Silver, & O'Brien, 1976). Children may use their illness and its treatment and management for various psychological purposes during different stages of development and different life situations. These purposes may include denial of illness, regression and passivity, hostility and punishment, assertion and rebellion, and other motives. A child may refuse to do prescribed body exercises, to maintain a modified diet, and to take necessary medication. Such behaviors are directed at the self and often at parents, physicians, and others in authority.

Somatic Behavioral Reactions

Another way in which stress may influence body function is through somatic reactions, a domain of behavioral reaction, as indicated in chapter 4. These include somatic pains, vomiting, enuresis (bedwetting), encopresis (soiling), constipation, tics, stuttering, and disturbances in body action or sensation. In some situations the body reaction symbolically represents the stressful idea and behavioral reaction. For example, vomiting may be an expression of disgust or rejection of an upsetting wish or idea, while a motor tic can be the compromise between the desire to be hostile and the inhibition of the hostile wish.

Body Image and Human Differences

There are also types of body image that can be stressful, since they represent painful departures from the imagined or real norms of physical appearance for children. They are often highlighted in adolescence. Body differences can be a focal point of teasing by other children. Children may view themselves as obese, thin, weak, short, tall, ugly, or otherwise negatively different. Feeling different in negative ways can result from minority-group status because of assumptions people make about language, ethnic, national, mental, behavioral, socioeconomic or other differences. For some children, wearing clothes different from the majority may be stressful.

An example will help to illustrate this.

• While making academic progress, Stan, age eight, was a behavior problem in the third grade. His behaviors centered on sexual actions toward classmates and sexual verbalizations to his teacher. Since the teacher was unable to contain these behaviors with limit setting and discussion or to clarify them with Stan's parents, she referred Stan to the school psychologist for further evaluation. The psychologist found out that Stan had been born with a small defect at the end of his penis (hypospadius), which the parents did not think needed surgical correction. Stan, however, could not urinate standing up because he would leak on the floor. He seemed very aware of his body differences from other children, as shown through his human figure drawings, which contained peculiarly shaped feet and toes, a reference to his own body differences. Unfortunately, the parents rejected the recommendation that they consult a pediatrician and psychiatrist for further assessment and consideration of plastic surgery. While Stan's sexual provocations diminished, he remained hyperactive and aggressive and had to be transferred to a classroom for emotionally impaired children.

Individual differences, represented by physical, mental, and emotional disabilities, may be experienced as stressful in relation to particular psychosocial contexts and consequences. They may be either visible or invisible differences. Such differences become accentuated in the context of regular, mainstream educational experiences, more extensive community contacts, further growth and development, and real as well as imagined stigmatized limitations in life activities. These issues are strongly influenced by socially determined stigma from able-bodied adults and children. It is here that teachers in regular and special classrooms can provide objective information about disabilities or differences, detoxify prejudicial and stigmatic attitudes and myths, and foster attitudes of acceptance of human differences among able-bodied and disabled children. Special education teachers also can better prepare disabled children in more segregated programs to deal with environmental experiences of prejudice that they are bound to face in the world.

Illness and Hospitalization

The experiences of illness, hospitalization, operation, and treatment may be stressful in themselves and create short- or long-term problems in adaptation (Blom, 1958). It has been estimated that 3.5 million children are admitted to hospitals every year and that every child has a fifty-fifty chance of being hospitalized once by the age of sixteen years (Shore, 1967). Such a high incidence provides schools with an opportunity to provide reactive interventions for children still undergoing stress from these experiences, as well as proactive efforts in anticipating a high-probability stressful event for other children. Parents, siblings, and relatives become ill, have operations, are hospitalized, may need ongoing treatment, develop disabilities and chronic illnesses, and sometimes die. These events also become sources of stress for schoolchildren.

The various experiences of illness are potential sources of stress to children, and the stress-intervention model presented in this book can be applied usefully in such situations. How well the direct and mediating factors balance one another will influence whether an event will be perceived as a challenge, a threat, a danger, or some combination of these. Such factors also function to facilitate or impede adaptation to stress.

Hospitalization

There have been changes in hospital and health professional policies and practices over the years so that greater sensitivity and psychological understanding are shown toward ill children and their parents. These include more liberal hospital visiting and realistic preparation of children for treatment and operative procedures (Shore, 1967). Hospitals at times can be environments freer of anxiety and guilt than home, and hospital staff can be sources of comfort and support not available in some families. Sometimes children feel supported by the company of fellow sufferers of their own age. On the other hand, hospitalization means separation from loved ones, friends, and familiar life routines, as well as exposure to alien, frightening, painful, unknown, and strange happenings and sights. Symbolically, it presents one of the earliest of life stressors: separation and strangeness.

Type of Illness

Another potential source of stress is the nature of the illness that the child has, that is, its severity, duration, amount of pain, body organ or part involved, real and imagined threats of injury and death, acuteness or chronicity, prognosis, and predictability or unpredictability of occurrence. For example, a child who is hospitalized for eye surgery because of a tumor will experience far more stress than the one having a tonsillectomy who is prepared ahead of time. Sudden, unpredictable injury tends to be more stressful than gradual, more predictable illness events.

Consequences of Illness

In addition to the illness, there are consequences that may also be as stressful or more stressful than the illness itself, such as treatment procedures. Being less able than most adults to connect cause and effect, children find it difficult to recognize that treatment, especially if it is painful or restrictive, is necessary for cure or improvement. Many times treatment measures such as immobilization, bed rest, limited diets, and injections bear some resemblance to past punishments and may be interpreted by children in that way. Other measures such as surgery, blood transfusions, dialysis, oxygen tents, and respirators are strange, frightening, and painful.

Let us consider an example of a child whose negative associations to his illness and to a surgical procedure that was contemplated were revealed to one of the authors (Blom, 1958).

> • Bobby, age eleven, was referred for evaluation because he felt dizzy, was extremely anxious, and appeared to be hyperventilating. He was hospitalized for the third time for operative correction of a knee deformity consequent to osteomyelitis (bone infection). He had been extremely fearful of surgery, particularly about being under anesthesia, which he thought might kill him.
>
> Bobby was the youngest of four children from a marginally stable family with siblings much older than himself. He was born when his mother was forty-five years of age. Because she already had begun menopause, the pregnancy was a surprise and unwanted. His osteomyelitis at age five and follow-up treatment were felt as an added burden by his parents. In his interviews, Bobby revealed the meanings of his illness and hospitalization through a discussion of the pigeons that

lived near his house. He particularly focused on an egg, which he repeatedly tried to get the mother and father pigeons to sit on. When
they refused to do this, he examined the egg. It smelled rotten so he
threw it in the garbage pail.

Our interpretation of this story is that Bobby felt like the rotten egg
that no one would care for, that was no good and should be thrown
into the garbage pail. This seemed to represent his fears of death and
concerns about lack of care and abandonment. Bobby was also at an
age when the concept of the finality of death would have developed.

A child's reaction to stressful events of illness will depend partially
on chronological and developmental age. Children frequently view
illness as punishment of wrongdoing and bad thoughts. They can be
helped if they are reassured by adults who are aware of such possibilities. The less-developed capacity of children for rational thinking
makes the assimilation of realistic information less certain. Illness may
be experienced as an attack or equivalent to other negative fantasies.
It is common, if not universal, for children to have fantasies about
their illnesses, treatments, and outcomes, both positive and negative.
The positive and negative fantasy balance, together with a rational
view, will influence how these experiences are perceived. Younger
children will react to the stress of separation, pain, and strangeness,
while older ones will be concerned about pain, multilation, harm, and
interruption in their lives. Adolescents may be concerned about being
different, losing control over their bodies, and the potential stigma of
disfigurement.

These stressful experiences may not have been fully processed and
assimilated by the time a child has returned to school. A few children
may return with disfigurement, bandages, casts, crutches, loss of hair,
and other noticeable changes. Children who have been absent have
often missed both academic learning and the social life of their classroom. They have fallen behind. When chronic illness persists, school
absenteeism may be an ongoing consequence that needs to be considered by the teacher.

Family Influences

Family factors will also influence whether illness events are stressful. Parents have their own anxieties about a child's welfare. They
may feel guilty and responsible for the illness, believing they should

have been more careful. This is particularly true for accidents. Parents may view illness as a reflection of their imperfection or as punishment for their own wrongs in the past or the present. Sometimes, as with children, guilt and punishment offer existential explanations for negative events. Usually the child who is ill receives more parental attention; over time, this can turn into overprotection. If this is prolonged, siblings may become angry and jealous and feel neglected and depressed. They also will be positively concerned about their ill brother or sister; and they will experience some sense of loss, since siblings in most families spend more time together than with any other family member. Chronic illness may place special stressors on the family that can result in financial problems, marital discord, more intense sibling reactions, and a different lifestyle for the family.

Here is an example that illustrates some of these points.

> • One first-grade boy, Jay, seemed his usual active and happy self at school but was slow and reluctant to leave the classroom at the end of the day. His teacher was puzzled by this change in behavior but was unable at first to find out anything from talking with Jay. She then phoned his mother, who was concerned not only about the welfare of her younger son who was hospitalized for cystic fibrosis but also about Jay's quiet, sad, inhibited behavior at home. Jay's mother was relieved that he was active and involved in school. With her permission, Jay's teacher talked to him after school the next day, mentioning that she knew about his sick brother. Jay took advantage of this opportunity to share his worries about his sick brother and how his parents were at the hospital all the time. From time to time Jay continued to initiate talks with his teacher. As a result, he seemed to be less reluctant in going home, due also to his mother's greater awareness of his needs, which she had temporarily forgotten.

Death

Death is another issue that comes to the attention of the child in the natural course of development and results in increasing recognition that living persons and other creatures die (Childers & Wimmer, 1971). This issue is often brought to children's attention by the death of a pet, a relative, or a relative of someone in the classroom, or through an exposure to illness on television. Eventually, children are confronted with the possibility of the death of their parents and their own death. This creates far more anxiety for the child as well as the adults who are asked for explanations. It is of course helpful and favorable for children to be introduced to death more gradually, through the dying of flowers, bugs, and pets. These represent inoculations that will help them to deal with more frightening losses later.

A child's view of death and the meaning ascribed to it changes in the process of development, from early concerns of being abandoned to later ones of being mutilated or damaged, to still later realistic ones of irreversibility and finality by about age ten or eleven (Anthony, 1971). There may be violent and painful associations to death, as well as symbolic personifications in the form of skeletons, monsters, and a person with a scythe. Children's reactions to death also depend upon the reactions and feelings of close adults. A child recognizes an adult's reactions and may be influenced positively by reassuring communication.

A century ago, when mortality rates were high, cultural views of death were more apparent. Death was ever present in people's prayers and in literature. As morbidity, mortality, and birth were controlled through technological advances, death became a more taboo topic. It is only in more recent years that talking and reading about death have become more common and at times somewhat excessive and faddish. It seems there are death workshops for everyone, including teachers and children. A more balanced perspective is one that responds to the concerns and questions of children as they develop and are exposed to death events in their peripheral and core lives.

Conclusion

Questions can be raised about the school's degree of responsibility in dealing with health-related stressors in children's lives. It is hoped that parents and health care professionals and agencies will take appropriate, helpful reactive and proactive interventions. Often, this does not happen, for a wide variety of reasons. It is inevitable that children will bring to school stress that affects their learning and social behaviors. Schools need to deal with these issues from the perspective that their primary function is education. At the same time, schools and teachers can be therapeutic without having to be treatment agencies or therapists.

12

School-Related Stressors

In addition to the primary goals of developing basic cognitive and linguistic skills and of imparting knowledge, another important goal of education is the socialization of children to the predominant values of society. This is done in collaboration with the family and other institutions of the community, hopefully with realistic mutual trust and confidence. References to socialization usually include its application to behaviors that require appropriate expression and control according to a large variety of individual and social contexts. One class of such behaviors is aggression.

Aggressive Behavior

There is considerable evidence that America and its schools may not be doing a very good job in socializing aggression in children (Center for Law and Education, 1978; Hyman & Wise, 1979; Olweus, 1978). Furthermore, hostile aggressive behaviors in schools are often sources of stress for children who attend them. These behaviors include peer bullying, antisocial peer pressure, teacher intimidation, threat and punishment, unruly classrooms and playgrounds, and destruction of school property. Violence in the schools against property and persons exists among children, between children and adults, and between parents and school personnel. Probably these forms of violence and destructiveness influence each other. Studies indicate that violence against school property and persons in a given school is related in part to the extent of corporal punishment existing at that school (Governor's Task Force on School Violence and Vandalism, 1978). It is also related to other factors that promote aggression within the school, community, and children's homes (Hyman & Wise, 1979).

The question of school violence and vandalism has been the object of both a national study (National Institute of Education, 1978) and a state study (Governor's Task Force, 1978). The National Institute of Education report indicated the nationwide nature of the problem, with financial cost to property amounting to $600 million per year. Over a five-year period, the study group found that the average school in the United States had a one-in-four chance of vandalism each month and a one-in-ten chance of burglary. Within a one-month period, a student had a one-in-nine chance of having something stolen, a one-in-eighty chance of being attacked, and a one-in-200 chance of being robbed. A teacher during a one-month period had a one-in-eight chance of having property stolen, a one-in-167 chance of being robbed, and a one-in-200 chance of being attacked.

The State of Michigan Task Force on School Violence and Vandalism (Governor's Task Force, 1978) reported findings from a sample of seventy school buildings in thirty-seven districts. Examples included broken windows, graffiti, textbook destruction, damage to school materials, and damage to property, as well as violence and aggression against children and adults. While the incidence varied from school to school, 5 percent of Michigan's two million schoolchildren displayed violence, truancy, fighting, drug use, and disciplinary problems. Factors that enhance and deter or control violence were examined in relation to students, educational personnel, families, and communities. Reasons for violence cited included the following:

1. Students were not participants nor included in the making of policies and decisions that affected them
2. Due process was rarely practiced by teachers and administrators
3. Authoritarian procedures were most common
4. Students often had to join groups for protection of self and property

Some students felt alienated from their school experience because of little help available from school staff and low expectations made of them. Parents felt overwhelmed by problems of unemployment and the raising of children. Exposure to media violence also was recognized as a contributor. School personnel expressed a need for protection as well as for effective management skills, even though their belief in a corporal punishment policy was prevalent. Administrators indicated a reluctance to report school crime because reporting crime might be viewed as an indication of their lack of competence. They also expressed a need for training in dealing with problems of aggression in schools and for networking help from community agencies. Communities were often unaware of school violence episodes and did not provide resource networks to deal with such problems. The many recommendations of the task force included developing a curriculum on violence, vandalism, and aggression for students, teachers, and administrators. Such a curriculum for students would involve both reactive and proactive intervention components for dealing with the receiving and expressing of aggression.

It must be emphasized that aggression is not a unitary concept; rather, there are different types of aggression, and it is important to distinguish them from each other since they have different implications for intervention. Four types of aggression can be identified: expressive, reactive, defensive, and assertive.

1. *Expressive aggression* represents a hostile urge or drive that begins to differentiate itself clearly during the second year of life. Its aim is destructiveness or power and is accompanied by pleasure in hurting, destroying, and displaying power. Regulation and modification of expressive aggression occurs through caring relationships and environments and the development of controlling and inhibiting mechanisms within the individual. Control and inhibition are usually first presented to the child by the caring environment and later, with maturation and experience, taken on by the child. Conflict arises between caring and destroying and functions as a barrier to expression.

2. *Reactive aggression* results from frustration, pain, punishment, restriction, humiliation, or deprivation of a child's wishes, intentions, and desires. It is associated with environmental happenings and is regulated by removing obstacles, increasing tolerance of frustration, improving skills in acquiring wishes and desires, and using alternative behavioral strategies in achieving desired goals. Some of these methods of regulation can be taught and modeled by others.

3. *Defensive aggression* is a hostile reaction against another feeling state, such as anxiety, that is uncomfortable and intolerable. Other uncomfortable feeling states may be depression, guilt, or even caring. Aggression develops because the other feeling state is threatening or dangerous. This defense has a biologically determined base in the alarm reaction for short-term dangers (Cannon, 1929) and the general adaptation syndrome (Selye, 1956) for prolonged stress. Identification of and tolerance for the underlying uncomfortable feeling state are ways in which defensive aggression can be regulated and modified.

4. *Assertive aggression* is nonhostile and involves energetic exploration of and learning about the world. These assertive behaviors are associated with mastery and problem solving and should not be identified as hostile in intent or feeling. Their expressions need encouragement that does not reinforce hostile aggression.

Regardless of the type of aggression, a teacher always contends with how it is expressed: physical action, body symptom, fantasy, drawing, writing, or verbalization. Important distinctions also exist about targets of aggression, such as a person, special parts of persons, self, and physical property. Schools often do not do a good job in making these distinctions and using them to judge an act's appropriateness to situational contexts for children. Controlled swearing in a child, for example, should be viewed as an advance over punching someone in the face and therefore not receive the same negative consequential response from a teacher.

The climate of aggression in schools provides a context for focusing on those forms of aggression that can be viewed as sources of stress for children. These are (1) corporal punishment in schools and (2) peer relations that include bullying and victimizing.

Corporal Punishment

While Americans are concerned about the high incidence of child abuse and neglect, they still accept corporal punishment in schools as public policy. It is a paradox that adult violence toward children is condoned in one area—school—while it is rejected in another area— home. In most states suspected or identified cases of child abuse and neglect legally must be reported by schools and other community agencies. However, the United States Supreme Court in 1977, in the case of *Ingraham* v. *Wright* (Center for Law and Education, 1978), made a decision on a five-to-four vote that corporal punishment in the school does not violate the eighth amendment to the Constitution, which prohibits cruel and unusual punishment. Furthermore, the court did not take a position about the lack of due process involved. In their decision, they affirmed the decisions of district and circuit courts. The *Ingraham* v. *Wright* case involved the Dade County School System, in which a fourteen-year-old boy was paddled twenty times by the school principal for having been slow in responding to teacher requests to leave the auditorium. Body injury and prolonged pain resulted. The case was a class action that included all students subjected to the corporal punishment policy of that school board.

As of 1985 there were seven states where corporal punishment was banned in schools (Satchell, 1985). Corporal punishment is a policy and action supported by editorial opinions in newspapers (McDonnell & Friedman, 1978) and by many parent and teacher groups, even though it is not practiced by many—probably the majority—of teachers in the schools where it is allowed. School corporal punishment is permitted in only two other Western nations, England and West Germany, while it is prohibited in most European democracies, communist nations, Japan, the Philippines, and some Arab nations. Punishment in schools supports the message of violence in our society, and of violence as a way of dealing with stress.

Corporal punishment in America has a background in Anglo-Saxon tradition and Judeo-Christian morality. It has been justified through questionable interpretations of such Biblical phrases as "spare the rod and spoil the child." There is a long history of officially sanctioned beatings of children in homes and schools, dating back to Colonial days. Teaching "to the tune of the hickory stick" endures. It is a practice of discipline justified by belief rather than by knowledge and assumed to lead to virtues of maturity, obedience, thrift, and righteous character. Moreover, there is the long-standing concept of the school serving "in loco parentis," or as substitute parents for children, an ancient credo dating from old common law. The justification of punishment is associated with public concern over discipline in school, a connection that has been confirmed repeatedly by Gallup polls (Gallup, 1978). Even with the advent of more humane methods of child rearing, children still have limited rights and are viewed as the property of parents and other adults.

There are very few reliable reports on the actual prevalence of school corporal punishment, which is defined as the infliction of pain, injury, confinement, or loss of personal freedom on a child as a penalty for the commission of some offense. Yet stories appear regularly and frequently in newspapers about such events, some of which may lead to legal suits alleging child abuse or other violations. During the 1971–72 school year, the school system of Dallas, Texas, recorded 24,305 paddlings in a school population of about 330,000, with unreported incidents probably being many times that number. In the 1972–73 school year, 46,022 cases of corporal punishment were reported in a study mandated by the California legislature; and during the first forty-five days of the 1975–76 school year in Miami, Florida, 2,892 paddling incidents were reported (Center for Law and Education, 1978).

A content analysis of 343 separate newspaper accounts of incidents of corporal punishment in schools has pointed to a number of surprising if not alarming findings (Clark, Liberman-Lascoe, & Hyman, 1980). Ninety-five percent of the offenses that led to corporal punishment were nonviolent, including truancy, smoking, poor grades, tardiness, cheating, swearing, chewing gum, or having one's shirttail out; only 5 percent of the offenses were classified as violent, such as fighting, pushing other children down, and pulling a chair out from under another child. The forms of punishment meted out by school authorities for either violent or nonviolent offenses were similar, and these retaliatory acts were far more aggressive than the original acts of disobedience of the child. Sixty-six percent of the time, children were punished by being paddled, strapped, or hit with objects. Thirty-five percent of the time, other methods of greater violence were used, such as pinching, kicking, taping the mouth of the child, requiring the child to run a gauntlet, standing on the child's toes, requiring the child to eat cigarettes, placing the child in a closet, choking, and dragging the child by the hair. Some of these forms of punishment resulted in nerve and tissue damage, fractures, blood clots, bruises, and other body damage, as well as emotional trauma.

Innumerable examples can be cited from newspaper accounts and court appearances (Hentoff, 1980). A fifth-grade boy was severely beaten on his back and buttocks for staying in the bathroom too long, because of constipation about which the teacher hadn't bothered to inquire. A fourth-grade girl was punched and shoved over her desk by a teacher for not being quiet. An eleven-year-old girl who was discovered chewing gum was paddled by her male teacher, who also directed her classmates to do the same to her. In general, boys are punished more than girls, and elementary schoolchildren more than secondary schoolchildren. Punishment is also used more frequently against emotionally disturbed, minority, and economically disadvantaged children.

We have had the opportunity to discuss corporal punishment in schools with groups of preservice and inservice teachers. In a nonjudgmental atmosphere they were encouraged to examine their views. There is a range of opinions and experiences that come out of such discussions. Some people assume corporal punishment is an option of the teacher that can be helpful; many parents at school conferences suggest that the teacher spank the child if needed; and some teachers use verbal abuse that may be even more detrimental than spanking. Some teachers distinguish between violent reactions toward a child and paddling used in a reasoned way. One student teacher indicated that she knew some principals who use corporal punishment but very appropriately. Another revealed that, even with a witness present, which was required, one teacher who was considered an excellent teacher beat a child with a ruler for four minutes. In some schools paddling has become the only way of dealing with misbehavior; in others, some teachers are afraid of being sued and do not use physical punishment. Another student teacher thought corporal punishment was very degrading to children, perhaps because it happened to her as a child and it was humiliating. Substitute teachers have been told to carry rulers for striking children. A first-grade boy was paddled for fighting by the principal, who said the punishment fit the crime.

These discussions frequently lead to the recognition by teachers of more rational alternatives to physical punishment and to appreciation of some of the negative consequences of physical force and of the need for more skills in classroom management. Most teachers and student teachers resisted the use of physical punishment, even when condoned within their school systems. Their childhood memories of such events were generally painful and upsetting, and viewing school corporal punishment in actuality or threat as a significant stress event in children's lives is enlightening for many teachers.

Peer Relationships

The interactions of children with their peers are influential in the social development of children and are often listed among the purposes of schooling in our society. For most children the give-and-take of working and playing with agemates is variously joyful and stressful. The process of finding one's place within a group, of learning to yield one's individual desires and interests to those of the group, and of developing enough self-confidence to oppose as well as accept group norms is clearly vital to the short- and long-term socialization of the child. It is argued sometimes that the school should not become involved in the socialization of children, but this is largely a false issue, as there is no way that such involvement can be avoided. The more pertinent concern is the extent to which teachers should exercise either reactive or proactive influence on the peer relationships that inevitably occur within their classrooms. Like it or not, the school must join the home, the church, and other institutions in sharing responsibility for the social development of children.

Peer relationships involve aggressive behaviors, competition, pressures to conform to agemate values, the formation of groups, sex-role experimentation, obtaining a more realistic appraisal of one's self, and the induction into the child culture. These are all issues in which the classroom teacher cannot always remain aloof and neutral. At times the teacher may need to intervene when events go awry and imbalances develop. Teasing, excessive competitiveness, bullying, and victimizing may occur.

Middle childhood is also a time when social acceptance from adults and peers is gained through the development and demonstration of realistic competencies. Children realize they are not loved or respected just for their existence, as in their own families. Outside their families, they have to gain or earn respect by demonstrating skills. Children without skills and competencies develop a sense of inferiority.

In primary school, children normally progress from predominantly egocentric behavior to involvement in groups of two or three. Loosely formed larger groups follow and tend to develop into strongly formed peer groups in late elementary and middle school years. Such groups become sources of emotional support, knowledge, values, and general cultural induction. In the worst instances they may foster normative behaviors and attitudes that are destructive to individual strengths and competencies. Fortunately, the overwhelming majority of children are able to maintain a reasonable balance between the demands of group membership and those for self-enhancement. Peer groups, for example, may exacerbate the tensions and power struggles that sometimes develop between children and adults, but most children maintain productive relationships with adults in spite of the excesses of some of their peers.

In our schools children are usually segregated by age and to some extent by sex. Age segregation is a matter of policy; sex segregation is more likely a matter of cultural influences. In the middle grades and preadolescence, boys tend to cluster together, and so do girls, even when they are showing growing awareness of the other sex. Teachers who wish to broaden the range of behaviors of both girls and boys may do so by encouraging cross-sex activities in the classroom. School activities that mix boys and girls may be expected to reduce stereotypic behavior and enhance mutual respect between the sexes.

There are some obvious advantages in grouping children by age. Limiting the range of individual developmental differences facilitates teaching and learning, social and emotional equality, and peer friendships. Age segregation also may lead to increased competition and aggression among peers, encourage generation gaps, and increase disrespect between age groups. School practices in which age groups are mixed for significant activities may encourage respect and friendship between children of different ages. The well-known advantages derived from asking older children to assist younger children with academic and manipulative skill-development activities support the claim for age-group mixing. It needs to be acknowledged, however, that older children who deliberately choose younger children as playmates and companions are sometimes viewed with suspicion in our age-segregated society. The older child whose preferred friend is younger may be suspected of being immature, insecure in the presence of peers, or, even worse, sexually deviant. Awareness of these possibilities may justify teacher attention, but not an assumption that the suspicions are inevitably true.

Among the most seriously damaging peer interactions are those of bullying and victimizing; hence they are areas that demand teacher attention. Bully and victim relationships are at the extreme end of the problems children experience in peer relations. They occur with some frequency in school as well as in the child's neighborhood and represent painful situations to many children. Myths and opinions exist among teachers and adults about bullies and victims. One of them is that victims are children who are "asking for it." Their behaviors and physical differences single them out as targets. They need to change their behaviors so as not to provoke aggression and must fight back in self-defense. Another myth is that bullies are expressing insecurity and usually grow out of their behaviors.

Olweus (1978) has studied bullies and victims in schools, including their interactions, their individual characteristics, and factors that tend to maintain victimizing behaviors. He has focused on boys who use both physical force and mental harassment on other children. The same phenomena exist with girls but have not been studied, although they have similar characteristics, except that with girls verbal and mental abuse tend to be more common than physical abuse.

As Olweus (1978) describes it, among boys in a class, there are normally some conflicts and tensions of different kinds. Usually there are frequent, slightly aggressive interactions, partly for fun, for self-assertion, and for the testing out of strength relationships among boys, much like establishing a pecking order. If there is a bully in such a group, the interactions will be rougher and more vehement and violent. The anger-prone temperament of the bully and his needs to assert himself and to dominate and subdue others are very evident in the classroom. Even minor adversities and frustrations result in intense aggressive reactions. Due to the physical strength of the bully, his attacks are often unpleasant and painful to others. Even if he attacks the weakest boys, whom he is certain of defeating, he is also not afraid of starting fights with other boys in the class. In general, he conveys toughness and self-confidence.

If there is also a whipping boy or victim in the class, he will soon be discovered by the bully. He is usually relatively passive, insecure, anxious, and unassertive; and he is often physically weak as well. The victim is the weakest link in the group, the one who does not retaliate when he is attacked, who becomes afraid and perhaps cries, and who is unwilling or unable to ward off attacks. Generally, he disapproves of taking part in rough games with the other boys of the class. As the class victim, he feels alone and isolated.

For a boy with bullying tendencies, the potential whipping boy is an ideal target victim. His anxiousness and defenselessness give the bully strong feelings of superiority, supremacy, and satisfaction of revengeful impulses. He concentrates his aggression on children who do not defend themselves. The bully usually wants to have others join him, and he induces them to pick on the whipping boy. There is usually something in the looks, clothing, or manners of the victim that can be the focus of attacks. It is equally as pleasurable for the bully to see other boys harass the whipping boy as it is to do it himself.

Adults at school frequently do not attend to these interactions and let these boys "settle their own conflicts." The boy victim usually does not protest to the teacher or to his parents. If he does, they often encourage him to deal with the problem himself.

Other boys in the class may also harass and tease the whipping boy. He is a safe target for attack, since he is weak and does not retaliate. None of the stronger boys in the class stand up for him. He is devalued and seems almost to deserve a beating. Gradually, the whipping boy becomes more isolated from his peers. His already low status is further impaired by teasing and attacks. Some boys are afraid of reducing their own status or of incurring disapproval by being seen with the whipping boy.

In any class, about 5 percent of the boys are clearly bullies and another 5 percent are victims (Olweus, 1978). A boy victim tends to have some externally observable characteristic that makes him different from most of the others, yet these characteristics are not unique to him. Victims, however, are physically weaker than the other boys, and they have not developed and used their strength. They are also nonaggressive, as determined by their anxiety and insecurity and by their fear of aggressive reactions from others.

Bullies are not necessarily different in external characteristics from other boys. They are not trying to compensate for some deviance or inferiority, but they tend to be much more aggressive, both physically and verbally, against peers and teachers. They value violence and violent means.

Evidence indicates that, three and five years later, the bullies and victims usually still display the same patterns of behavior (Olweus, 1978). They are not outgrown and usually remain stable. Children in the class tend to admire the bully and despise the victim and develop group norms that permit bullying and victimization. These developments occur because the negative interaction is ignored and is thought to be a behavior that will be outgrown, and group norms against bullying are not established and maintained by the teacher. Still later in the school experience the bully's popularity decreases so that he receives less positive reinforcement. He is left with an aggressive behavior pattern with no positive consequences.

Teachers should intervene individually with both bullies and victims, as well as foster positive peer group norms. Bullies may be offered other forms of power and leadership and should receive negative consequences for their aggression. Increased capacity for empathy should be fostered. Victims can be encouraged to be assertive and to have an increased tolerance of suffering; they need to have competencies other than those that rely on physical powers.

Children with Disabilities

Children with disabilities present stress issues in many forms, especially the stress of going to and attending school from a more protected home environment, the interaction with able-bodied children, and the exposure of able-bodied children to those who are mentally and physically different. Parents and teachers share in these sometimes stressful events.

The prevalence of disabled children has been estimated at 7.8 million, about 12 percent of the child population (American Education Reprint, 1976). This total may be broken down to show the following numbers of children by disability category:

Speech impaired	2,293,000
Mentally retarded	1,507,000
Learning disabled	1,966,000
Severely emotionally disturbed	310,000
Health impaired and physically impaired	328,000
Hearing impaired	377,000
Visually impaired	66,000
Multiply handicapped	40,000

With the advent of the mandatory special education act of 1975 (PL94–142), these children for the most part are being provided services in public schools in both segregated and integrated settings. There is also considerable pressure to provide appropriate mainstream experiences for these children.

Robert Louis Stevenson is reported to have said, "Life is some-times not a matter of holding good cards but of playing a poor hand well." School professionals can contribute a significant role in the fa-cilitation of playing the poor hand well. Another role is to limit the handicap so that it does not extend to other areas of development. With the severely handicapped, the school helps share the burden with parents by providing respite care as well as by teaching tech-niques and procedures for the care of their children. For the child, care and teaching at school often provide an atmosphere freer from stress and tension than what may exist at home.

In the younger child, courage and struggles to master can be ad-mired, dependency is more acceptable, behavioral management is usually easier, and physical attractiveness is less of an issue. But in adolescence, friendships, sexuality, employment, and the adult rec-ognition of being different become difficult, stressful issues for dis-abled persons, their families, and the professionals who work with them. There is often an avoidance among teachers in dealing with these issues at older age levels. However, when school programs have staffs that can share concerns, puzzlement, and frustration, difficult tasks are lessened and can be anticipated. If there are professionals from other disciplines available, they can make contributions to the ongoing problem-solving tasks.

Cultural and Historical Attitudes Toward Disability

In spite of education and training, teachers and other child profes-sionals are still influenced by societal prejudices and cultural atti-tudes concerning disability. This may exist at a conscious level but is sometimes less conscious. When these attitudes remain less conscious and denied, then it may be difficult to modify them and their influ-ences. Throughout history to the present, there have been cultural beliefs about death, illness, and handicap. Handicaps were fre-quently a tabooed, feared, avoided, and denied subject. The problem is that such attitudes still exist today in more muted forms, and they influence the interpretation of events in the lives of the disabled.

As we mentioned in an earlier chapter, death, prevention of ill-ness, and recovery from sickness were prominent themes in the prayers, precepts, stories, and children's books of our society a cen-tury ago. Infirmity, childhood morality, old age, handicap, and illness were acknowledged as part of life. *McGuffey's Fourth Eclectic Reader* (1879) dealt with the dangers of drowning and fires, warnings, infirmity, old age, chronically ill parents, physically handicapped children, child illness, a child being lost, laziness, hazing of children, poverty, lost animals, a mother's grave, and other issues. Such topics might be considered somewhat of a heavy dose of stark reality these days. The stories also had moral overtones, presenting bad fates often as a consequence for bad acts. However, they did deal with realities in some people's lives and the lives of some children. Children were not overprotected and denied recognition of such events. This is to be contrasted with the content of modern-day schoolbooks, which systematically avoid both the natural differences among people as well as their sometimes unhappy events and fates (Zimet, 1975).

So there is much in our culture that conspires, from an early age, against the appropriate acknowledgment, acceptance, and discussion of disabled children. That this is not easily modified at older ages and by further education is suggested by a study of able-bodied adults, on social distance toward handicapped persons (Tringo, 1970). The findings of this study show a trend for hidden handicaps such as ulcer, asthma, diabetes, and heart disease to be more acceptable than visible ones such as dwarfism, cerebral palsy, hunchback, and mental retardation.

Disability Today

Various irrational views, handicap labels, and negative practices still exist in the care and education of disabled children, contributing further to the disability's stressful character. Although positive changes have occurred, including less isolation and segregation of the handicapped and the elimination of offensive terms such as moron, imbecile, and idiot, the experiences of the disabled at school and in the community are still controlled and restricted. In attempts to mainstream disabled children appropriately, schools, teachers, parents, and able-bodied children are often not prepared to accept those who are different. Parents of disabled children may fear that their child will not be protected in such surroundings. Handicapped children can become objects of ridicule, attack, and rejection. Their disturbed behavioral responses may be less tolerated by others. Able-bodied children may react with anxiety and discomfort to disabled children. However, there are also teachers and schools who prepare for these developments and deal with them effectively. As normalization as a humanistic principle is developed and promoted, preparation and clarification for all involved parties are necessary. The principle of normalization needs to be understood, not feared. It is defined by Wolfensberger (1972) as using means as normative as possible to establish or maintain behaviors and characteristics of life that are as culturally normative as possible. The key words are "as possible." Nirje (1969), a Swedish psychologist, defines normalization similarly, that is, the process of making available to handicapped people patterns and conditions of everyday life as close as possible to the norms and patterns of the mainstream of society.

Going to School

Going to and attending school present a series of tasks and experiences in which a number of challenges, stressors, and changes are presented. This is true for all children but is highlighted for the disabled child. There are the emotional tasks of relating to other peers and adults, more separation and independence from the family, coping with newness and anxiety, and a focus on the development of skills and achievements through instruction and practice.

For some disabled children the transition from a family- and home-centered environment to school proceeds with limited difficulty or with transitory difficulties. These children may have had previous experiences in the care of adults other than parents that have been favorable. However, such favorable factors do not exist for some disabled children. Some of them have been overchallenged with too many expectations or ones that are too difficult and inappropriately timed. Others have not been challenged enough.

A disabled child may have been overprotected and indulged, without sufficient limit setting. As a result this child may lack the freedom, comfort, and inner resources needed for engaging new situations and expectations at school. At the other extreme a child may not have received sufficient protection and guidance at home and been expected to negotiate without help. Such a child may find the school expectancies strange, different, and overwhelming. In both extremes these children have discordant school and home experiences. These kinds of discrepancies will present stressful events for the child unless they are clarified and modified.

As with all children, there are stressful life experiences that impinge on the handicapped child and family and influence the child's reactions to school life; most notably, (1) family moves; (2) death or illness in family members; (3) parent separation and divorce, which are higher in families with handicapped children; (4) a birth of a sibling; and (5) parent unemployment. However, some disabled children may find in school more stability, predictability, and consistency than exist at home.

Family-School Relations

Parents of disabled children may bring to the school situation their own problems, anxieties, and conflicts. Frequently, their own negative childhood experiences in relation to learning, schools, and teachers become activated through the problems of their own child. If the handicapped child shows little progress, parents can be caught in a web of anxieties, resentment, and guilt. It is not easy for the school to avoid being defensive, to sort out what is rational and irrational about parent complaints, and to deal with parental reactions in constructive ways.

Home visits by school personnel and school visits by parents may bridge the gaps in understanding and foster alliances for problem solving. However, when family members and/or school personnel feel threatened, mistrustful, defensive, and blamed, visits and contacts will be dominated by negative feelings, so that building an alliance will be difficult.

Parents of handicapped children may not recognize the circumstances, problems, and difficulties that schools and their teachers must confront. They may not have a realistic understanding of the child's disability and of what can reasonably be expected. Schools are frequently scapegoated for slow progress. They may become targets of displaced parental frustration, anger, and despair just because schools are so readily available.

School professionals may view disturbed behaviors of handicapped children as being simply the result of family experience and child rearing. This viewpoint does not sufficiently recognize that the handicapped child is a unique individual who responds to both the inner developing world and outer events in particular ways. The stresses of life are compounded for parents by having a child with a disability. Greater demands on parents result. Under such circumstances families may not display the strengths, resources, and capacities that schools expect them to have. To attend school meetings, to take a child to a physician or clinic, or to schedule a home visit may mean loss of income and leaving other children at home unattended. It is not that expectations and responsibilities should not be made of parents; rather, they need to be done in realistic and empathic ways that consider the nature of their lives.

Staff Relations

It is understandable that school staff will have reactions to handicapped children. It helps if the school staff members can assess, without guilt, their own reactions as individuals, share them with trusted colleagues or teams, and ensure that rewards and pleasures come from their own personal lives. There may be specific handicaps that bother a teacher the most or behaviors that are especially uncomfortable. Judgments can develop in relation to unwed mothers, alien family lifestyles, forms of parent discipline and child rearing, and lack of cleanliness. It is easy for those who work with children to compete with parents and to overidentify with the child.

The school represents an introduction to and preparation for the world of reality. While the school offers support to the disabled child and family, its goals are to foster and develop skills and capacities that promote adaptation and normalization as realistically as possible. This means recognition of what is possible and not possible for an individual child. It requires a balance of empathic and objective attitudes toward the handicapped child as well as multifaceted skills on the part of school staff. Schools are both influenced and restrained by the intentions of the larger society of which they are a part. One of the challenges of the school is to develop an ongoing working alliance with the disabled child and the family. Difficulties arise between family and school, and incongruencies exist. Different issues develop over time, requiring new decisions to be made. Time is required for those problem-solving efforts. School staff have reactions to handicapped children that require self-awareness and sometimes the support of trusted members on the school staff in order to restore a realistic and humanistic, workable perspective.

Academic Pressure and Excessive Competition

Among those potential stressors commonly related to schooling are the pressures associated with academic demands and stemming from excessive competition among children. It is not at all uncommon for these two potential stressors to be closely related. Obviously some of these pressures are created and exacerbated by the home influences and the larger society. Teachers need to be sensitive to the amount of pressure being exerted on each child and the ways each child responds to such pressure. At the very minimum, teachers should be particularly aware of the extent to which teacher expectation and behavior contribute to stress in children.

Teachers set expectations, and these tend to be somewhat self-fulfilling. For example, a teacher who expects to be obeyed is more likely to be obeyed than one who does not. Teachers can reduce the potential stressors present in the classroom by

1. Adjusting behavior limits to reflect the development of greater maturity, independence, and responsibility in children
2. Emphasizing positive expectations
3. Demonstrating an instructional approach to socialization rather than a restrictive or punitive approach
4. Explaining the reasons for demands made on children
5. Helping children to understand the implications of their behavior, for their own well-being
6. Consistently adjusting and enforcing behavioral rules
7. Modeling the behaviors expected of children

Some teachers intentionally or unwittingly maintain a social stratification by creating a caste system that may continue through several grade levels. For example, it is probable that some primary children are assigned to reading groups according to subjective impressions about their likelihood of success in school, and these impressions often reflect a social-class bias. This caste system may be perpetuated by middle-grade teachers. Teachers, many of whom come from middle-class homes, almost inevitably impose middle-class norms in assessing students. Punctuality, neatness, deference to authority, and academic skills are examples of traits valued by the middle class. Consequently, teachers should continually monitor their own attitudes and behaviors as they work with those children who display fewer academic skills, less orderly behavior, and less acceptance of adult authority.

Homework can be the source of considerable stress in some children, especially when coupled with a parent or parents who set unreasonably high standards for their children. Allen is a case in point.

• Allen was a sixth grader in Mrs. George's room who expressed great dismay and disapproval when Mrs. George assigned homework to be completed for the following day. By talking privately with him, she tried to find out why Allen was so upset by homework assignments. She found him very uncommunicative; all he would say was that he did not like to take home work to be completed.

At the next parent/teacher conference, Mrs. George told Allen's mother of his reaction to homework. Allen's mother informed Mrs. George that Allen's father held the opinion that Allen should be able to get his work done at school, so, to avoid being physically punished, Allen often came directly home from school to do his homework before his father came home from work around 6 P.M. This meant that Allen did not have time to play with his friends after school or to stay after school on the two days each week that the school sponsored an organized sports program. Allen's mother also confided that he had received numerous paddlings when he was in fifth grade, for doing homework after dinner.

As a reactive intervention measure, Mrs. George worked with Allen over the next few weeks, to help him organize his school day so that he could get most if not all of his homework done during the school day. She also began to think of a way she could approach Allen's father about the value of homework and to tell him that the amount of Allen's homework was likely to increase as he progressed into higher grade levels.

Teachers need to be sensitive to the interactions that regularly occur between school policies and practices and the expectations of parents. Allen's homework problem is a good example of the kinds of stressors that are generated between home and school.

Even in elementary school, paper-and-pencil testing situations also can be a source of stress in children. Those children who are anxious a great deal of the time, those who do not do well on tests generally, and those who are excessively competitive often suffer greater anxiety around test time. Most children experience test anxiety to some extent at some time, and low levels can act as a motivator for some children, but high levels of anxiety seriously interfere with children's test performances.

Teachers can do a number of things to reduce the stress some children associate with tests. A test should usually not be a surprise to the class. Tests should be announced well in advance, including the material to be tested, the exact nature of the test, and the significance of the test in the overall grading plan. Children should be taught how to study for and take tests, and they should be allowed to practice on test items that are similar in construction to the actual test items. Kesselman-Turkel and Peterson (1981) and Large (1978) offer a number of sound suggestions for preparing students to take tests, as well as techniques for taking tests that elementary teachers can teach to middle- and upper-grade children.

Excessive competition among children need not be the norm in the elementary classroom. Teachers can structure both the academic environment and playground and gym activities in ways that minimize competition. Slavin's (1980) work on cooperative learning describes a number of techniques that structure school activities so that cooperation among children is rewarded and competition is not. Slavin found cooperative learning to be characterized by higher achievement at all ability levels and by a focus on academic learning. Noncognitive outcomes of cooperative learning activities include a higher degree of cooperation among participants across race, sex, and age differences; a mutual concern for others in the group; more cross-racial choices of participants; and better acceptance of impaired children who were mainstreamed.

Family Mobility

American families are on the move. The children in families that move must usually leave one school and enroll in another. Many children do this more than once during the elementary school years. If the two schools are in the same community, the transition may be only somewhat less difficult than if the schools are in different communities. The associations of elementary schoolchildren tend to be limited to playmates and classmates who live in their immediate neighborhoods and who attend their schools. A school only five miles down the road is as "foreign" to the child as one fifty or 500 miles away, in many respects.

Parents have reasons for moving their families, and the nature of their reasons affects their moods, enthusiasm, and preparation for moving. Parents who are moving for reasons of unemployment, family illness, death, divorce, or separation are likely to have a different influence on their children than those who are moving to improve their living conditions. Parents who remember their own childhoods and who themselves are pleased to be moving may be sensitive to the needs of children, allaying their fears and encouraging their positive acceptance. Even under these favorable circumstances the move requires the child to leave friends and find a niche among strangers. The process of identifying and developing a new role that is acceptable to the child and respected by the new peers is not without complications.

Childhood competitiveness directed at a newcomer may go beyond challenge and become fear inducing as children test each other in the process of getting acquainted and assuming new roles within the group. The child whose self-perception includes being different or inferior may have a particularly difficult transition. Usually the difficulties of adjustment are more perceived than real but not always. In either case, the influence of significant adults who wish to be supportive and intelligently reassuring can smooth the way for the uprooted child.

Most schools gain and lose some students during an academic year. This is known as the *mobility rate* for a school and is computed by dividing the total number of children entered and withdrawn in a school year by the average daily school enrollment. Mobility rates will vary by regions of the country, employment patterns in communities, socioeconomic conditions, and other factors.

In one metropolitan school district with forty-three elementary schools, Blom (1980b) found that the mean rate of school mobility was 33.7 percent, with a range of 15.5 percent to 69.4 percent. Comparing the family forms found among the four elementary schools with the lowest mobility rates and the four elementary schools with the highest mobility rates, Blom found that in the high-mobility schools there were almost twice as many families with the mother as head of household (42.1 percent) as there were in the low-mobility schools (22.7 percent). Such a finding is not surprising, as it is well known that employment patterns and family financial conditions in mother-headed households tend to be less adequate and stable than in two-parent and father-headed homes, on the average.

In a feature story on divorce, *Newsweek* (Divorce American Style, 1983) declared that "divorced women with children have become the nation's new poor." This situation is the result of a combination of factors that include divorce settlements in which alimony is seldom awarded, joint custody arrangements that are not workable, child support payments ordered but not paid, inequitable salaries for women, late entrance of women into the workforce, and lack of training and skills in the higher paying occupations. These are examples of variables that place single women and their children among the high-mobility-rate families.

Student mobility adversely affects academic achievement. Kealey (1981) administered the SRA Achievement Test to 1,882 seventh-grade students in forty-three Catholic elementary schools in Manhattan and the Bronx. A nonmobile group of students consisting of 41.3 percent of the population had been in one school since first grade, while the remaining 58.7 percent had changed schools at least once. The children who had not changed schools outscored the others in reading by an average of one year and three months. Kealey concluded that remaining in the same school has a positive effect on achievement in reading and mathematics.

What can teachers do to ease the stress that many children experience when they move? For children who are leaving the classroom, it would be well to discuss the matter with the child, sharing personal experiences and listening to the child's account of his or her own feelings. If it is known where the child will be enrolling, it would be especially helpful to send a personal note to the teacher or principal of the new school, introducing the child to these important adults. Classmates who have recently moved may be able to make reassuring comments about their experiences. A children's book that tells an appropriate story about a child entering a new school or neighborhood might be helpful in allaying fears. It would be consistent with the advice of Brooks (1982) to provide assurances that members of the class will send letters over the first few weeks or months and to request that the child write in return, describing new friends, teachers, and activities. She indicates that a smooth transition usually results if ties are permitted to endure for a while after a child has moved. A party for the child who is leaving may do a lot to say, "we will miss you."

Similarly, the teacher who is receiving a new student may do simple things to welcome the child that will put some fears to rest. The child's introduction to new classmates may be crucial in setting the tone that they will adopt in relating to the newcomer. Careful exploration of the child's skills and attitudes toward school will help in making the appropriate placement within the class. Some thought given to the children with whom the new child is placed for initial activities might help inform the child of the behavioral expectations of the class. A parent-teacher conference as early in the transition period as possible is certainly crucial. Helping the parents feel welcome and informing them about the concerns for their child's smooth adjustment should help to convey a positive message about the new school. Acknowledgment of the child's feelings of loneliness, apprehension, and strangeness is likely to be reassuring. Group activities that encourage acceptance of the newcomer by classmates may have the reciprocal effect of helping the unacquainted one like the group.

Smoothing the path for the child who has moved requires little more than remembering one's own childhood and acting sensitively to allay the fears remembered and to facilitate the building of needed relationships.

Conclusion

A wide range of potential stressors, both acute and chronic, occur in school settings. Yet, they may not receive appropriate teacher attention compared to stressors in the out-of-school lives of children. It is usually easier for professionals to identify and examine events and practices outside of the system they belong to. We have found that teachers tend to first identify sources of potential stress in settings outside of school before recognizing stressors occurring at school. In this chapter school stressors have been examined in relation to various school issues and practices such as corporal punishment, peer relationships, children with disabilities, academic pressure and excessive competition, and student mobility.

13

Children Who Cope

Principals and teachers have known many children who have coped with stress and adversity in their lives and obtained life satisfactions in spite of these unfavorable circumstances. Some of these children can be described as "doing remarkably well," but not much is known about their psychological characteristics or the mechanisms by which they cope. Furthermore, the frequency with which children successfully cope with adversity is not generally known either.

Mental health professionals have tended to focus their attention on those who are not coping and not leading adaptive and satisfying lives. Using this biased selection of persons with psychological symptoms and problems, generalization of findings from a minority have been made to other people in similar situations and circumstances. This interest in psychopathology has skewed impressions on how the majority of persons deal with acute and chronic stress in their lives.

Empirical Studies

In the last twenty years psychiatrists and psychologists have reported findings on children exposed to situations that put them at risk for the negative consequences of stress. These situations have included a range of environmental and individual adverse circumstances such as having parents with chronic mental or physical illness (Anthony, 1975; Bleuler, 1974; Garmezy, 1974), living in inner-city low-income neighborhoods with high delinquency rates (Garmezy, 1981); Neuchterlein, 1970; Rutter, 1979), living in racially prejudiced and rejecting communities (Coles, 1964), having physical disabilities, and being exposed to other acute and chronic stress situations (Blom, 1984). While the children in these studies had a somewhat higher percentage of adjustment difficulties than those in the general population, the majority (close to 85%) adjusted satisfactorily. Of this majority group, 5 to 10 percent did remarkably well and have been referred to as "invulnerables," "superkids," or "children who will not break." A more objective term for these children is "stress resistant."

Longitudinal developmental studies of "normative" children (Harris, 1959; Murphy & Moriarity, 1976; Werner & Smith, 1982) also have identified children who were particularly resilient to stressful life events and responded to individual or environmental difficulties as challenges to be overcome. Resilience, coping, and stress resistance have been identified as normative forms of the adaptive response to unfavorable endowment, environment, or events. These can be added to the more familiar normative forms of less-adaptive and maladaptive responses, such as vulnerability, defending, fragmenting, and psychopathology.

Another source of supportive evidence for coping is the naturally occurring examples in everyday life, presented in newspaper and other media accounts, of children who respond with heroism and other positive behaviors when confronted with acute and chronic stress. Many times their responses are considered remarkable, outstanding, astounding, or inspirational, because they are adaptive beyond the expected range. A partial list of newspaper headlines of stories about children's heroism, problem solving, and other coping with difficulty includes the following:

> Active Teenager Deals with Deafness
> Kids, Waiting to Die, Learn How to Live
> Hero, Age 3, Frees Parents and Cop
> Babysitter Rescues Child, Puppy
> Girl Escapes from Abductor's Car Trunk
> Girl Stops Car to Save Mom, Sister
> Youth Who Doused Fire Said He Didn't Have Time for Fear
> Bootless, Little Food, 4 Survive

Over the last three years a list of thirty-two randomly selected stories of a similar nature has been collected (Blom, 1984). A content analysis of these accounts points to these children as being ready to help others, adjusting to novel or unusual situations, planning their behaviors, thinking creatively, being optimistic, tolerating intense emotions, being aware of their power to influence life events, and being altruistic. This information is brought to the attention of teachers since it is readily observable in most classrooms and provides common-sense validation of the characteristics of children who cope.

Definitions of Coping

The empirical evidence for a paradigm of coping is supported by various dictionary definitions that present considerable thematic similarity. To cope means to contend, strive, and struggle; to encounter or overcome problems and difficulties on even terms or with success. In chapter 5 psychological definitions of coping were presented as well, particularly some of its behavioral characteristics and the distinctions between coping, defending, and fragmenting.

White (1979) considers coping to be new behavior that develops when a given problem defies a familiar way of responding to it. Coping is stimulated when a person meets difficult and unfamiliar situational requirements. It includes behaviors that are contending, striving, persisting, resisting, and opposing. It consists of an active psychological effort to overcome, master, and solve internal (personal) and external (environmental) problems and dilemmas. According to Murphy (1981), both coping and defending processes are used by children to overcome stress. Coping involves elasticity and creative restructuring of tasks, challenges, obstacles, and frustrations. Coping individuals also need to experience positive feedback or similar reactions from others in their environment. Garmezy (1981) describes coping as a pattern of behavioral responses to novel situations, obstacles, and conflicts in which search, effort, direct action, and shaping of events occur. From the standpoint of all the previously cited authors, then, coping can be viewed as learned behavior that can perhaps be generated through instructional and therapeutic endeavors.

Stress-Resistant Children

A model for identifying, processing, and intervening in the stress events that occur in the lives of children has been presented. The interventions represent reasonable expectations that can be made of teachers, even given the already large number of demands placed upon them. The intervention process is seen as contributing to the learning of skills and knowledge as well as facilitating behavior management in the classroom. A natural extension of stress intervention is derived from the potential that our observations of children who cope present to us for the development of strategies that generate adaptive behavior responses in all children.

Several researchers have reported behavioral characteristics of stress-resistant children, mostly those at risk from chronic stressful environmental situations (Anthony, 1974; Bleuler, 1974; Coles, 1964; Garmezy 1974; Rutter, 1979; Segal & Yahraes, 1978). These characteristics can be organized into the social, cognitive, affective, and self domains. Socially, these children are described as personable, sensitive to the feelings and needs of others, empathic, well liked by peers and adults, verbally fluent, well behaved in classrooms, and ready to help others. Often a nonfamily adult such as a teacher is important in their lives.

In the cognitive realm, stress-resistant children think for themselves, have good attentional processes, are problem solvers, are reflective and resourceful, and they make creative use of imagination and fantasy. Information is employed effectively, and they do well in novel situations. They test reality well and can distinguish between reality and fantasy.

Affectively, these children have capacities for frustration tolerance and gratification delay. They achieve a balance in emotional expression and control, are optimistic, and have a sense of humor.

Their self characteristics include positive self-regard, self-esteem maintenance, internal locus of control, and appropriate acceptance of responsibility. They resist negative labels and do not assume a victim identification. They often have special interests and activities, in addition to liking school and people.

Studies of Children Who Cope

From 1979 through 1983, many of our graduate students who are teachers have interviewed children as part of their coursework on stress and coping; as a result, many coping children have been described. These children were singled out because they did very well under adverse circumstances or chronically stressful events. After obtaining school, parent, and child consent, these children were interviewed at school, following a procedure in which each child first ranked eight topics in the order in which the child preferred to discuss them. The child then talked about these topics in the selected order, with some guidance from the interviewer. Further information was obtained about the children from their parents and teachers, including stress inventories and behavior checklist data. Twelve of these children are identified as follows:

> Sixteen-year-old girl with muscular dystrophy
> Fifteen-year-old boy with mild mental retardation and speech disorder
> Fourteen-year-old girl with congenital blindness
> Twelve-year-old girl in a family with schizophrenic parents
> Eleven-year-old French boy attending school in the United States
> Ten-year-old Native American boy in a foster home
> Ten-year-old boy with a learning disability
> Ten-year-old boy who was a hero during a school disaster
> Ten-year-old boy moving to England, away from his mother
> Nine-year-old boy with family divorce and a new stepfather
> Eight-year-old boy from the inner city, with many recent stresses
> Eight-year-old girl with progressive genetic blindness

All of these children were either completely or partially mainstreamed in school. They came from intact as well as nonintact families, and their experiences with parents were not always optimal. The children clearly identified the acute and chronic stress conditions operating in their lives. When complete data were obtained, life stress scores were high, as were prosocial behavior ratings on behavior checklists. Interviewer ratings of coping dimensions were also high, confirming their effectiveness in coping with adversity.

For ten of the twelve children studied, information about their rank-ordered selection of topics for discussion is presented in table 13.1. Of particular interest are the high rankings on other-directed, reality-based topics, as compared to the low rankings on inner-directed, more subjective topics. This reflects their active dealing with the world of people and things, rather than withdrawal and inner preoccupations.

TABLE 13.1 *Order of Selection of Topics by Preference for Discussion*

Topic	Mean of Order of Selection
School	2.4
Friends	3.1
Interests/Activities	3.3
Imagination/Wishes	3.6
Myself	3.8
Home/Families	4.0
Future	5.2
Worries/Feelings	5.5

A content analysis of transcribed interviews was done, to identify behavioral characteristics of the twelve children. It was found that these children tend toward the following behaviors:

1. Attract and use the support of adults at home and school
2. Have a future orientation with realistic goals
3. Are sensitive, empathic, and insightful about their environments and other people
4. Are inner directed, think autonomously, and desire privacy
5. Clearly identify what is least and most liked about their lives
6. Use fantasy creatively and distinguish it from reality
7. Are friendly, personable, talkative, and at ease
8. Experience the support of at least one stable significant adult
9. Can detach from the dysfunctional behaviors of others
10. Succeed in and like school and are liked by peers
11. Are self-reliant and believe they can control life events
12. Do not view themselves with the negative labels assigned by others

This list of characteristics does not give a complete, integrated picture of what these children were like. The following summarized examples of some specific children help to capture that.

• Caroline is a sixteen-year-old girl with muscular dystrophy who is a wheelchair user. Both parents are in good health, but one of her brothers also has muscular dystrophy. Overall, Caroline is optimistic, cheerful, and self-reliant. She expresses a measure of regret over her disability but does not think about it much, despite the fact that a close friend died of the disorder. Caroline says she and her parents do not always get along, because she feels they are overprotective. Yet they do allow her to have a part-time job and are supportive of her college plans. She has both handicapped and nonhandicapped friends and plays wheelchair hockey. She does well in school and hopes to be a counselor for children when she grows up.

• Joe, a fifteen-year-old ninth grader, has received special education services for six years. While categorized as educable mentally impaired, he has always been mainstreamed in some general education classes. For example, in ninth grade he takes woodshop and world history, both of which require passing written exams. In addition to the frustration of his slow academic progress, Joe is in his first year of high school, where he has been exposed to some bullying. Additional life stressors include an unmarried sister's pregnancy, parents' separation, father's inconsistent employment, and a friend who drowned the previous summer. Joe is viewed by school people as a likeable person who works hard, often at a level above his supposed ability. He is socially at ease and uses teachers for appropriate help and support. He responds to and enjoys challenges. He is an achiever and feels he is responsible for the way his life turns out and therefore plans long-term goals.

• Susan, age twelve, is the oldest of three children in a family with multiple problems. She has a bright, schizophrenic younger brother; a paranoid, angry father; a schizophrenic, overly religious mother; and a schizophrenic, agitated maternal grandmother. Her parents are divorced. Susan attends sixth grade in a middle school. Her life there is relatively problem free, and she is liked by both peers and teachers. Susan is a peacemaker between her mother and maternal grandmother, who argue a good deal. She has a sense of caring for the upset people in her household but maintains some emotional distance and objectivity toward them. This means she disconnects from their abnormal behaviors and responds to her own reality testing of what is appropriate and sensible. She accepts nurturance and guidance from her mother when it appears appropriate. Susan would like her family to function normally, but she can accept the times when it does not and obtain satisfaction when it does. She also finds fulfillment and caring outside the family setting.

• Hal is ten years old and the eldest of three boys in a stable and religious family. He is in the sixth grade and is a member of the school safety patrol. He was cited for heroism by several public institutions, for his actions during a school disaster involving an elevated crosswalk. Several children were injured, yet Hal remained calm and collected throughout the whole ordeal. This is but one illustration of his maturity, sensitivity, and intelligence. Hal does well in school, has many friends, and is active in a number of extracurricular activities. He has a positive self-image and is empathic with others. He enjoys problem-solving activities.

• Laurence is eleven years old and is the eldest of the two boys in his family. Recently, the family moved to Michigan from France, for a two-year visit. His principal noted Laurence's lack of the usual behavioral symptoms associated with a major upheaval of this type. Laurence is an outgoing, talkative young man who comes from a supportive home environment. He is able to express himself well in English, despite having only limited experience with the language. He feels challenged to succeed and views himself favorably in relation to his peers. He sees himself as a protector of his younger brother and the one who takes care of his mother when his father is away from home.

• Johnny, a ten-year-old Native American boy, attended fifth grade in a school a great distance from his community school on the reservation. He had been placed in a foster home three months earlier because of drinking problems and marital discord in his family. Johnny did average academic work and got along well with adults and classmates at school. He apparently also did well in the school on the reservation. Johnny had many ongoing stress events in his life—problem drinking, marital instability, minority status, foster home placement, and a change in school—yet he seemed to respond to them as situations to be overcome. Johnny had been placed in the same foster home and attended the same school in second grade, so the placement was familiar and he had adjusted well before. Johnny explained it this way: "I have two homes; when things get bad with my mother at home, I can come here; when it gets better at home, I can go back."

• Nancy is eight and one-half years old. She has been visually impaired since birth. Her impairment has been progressive, and blindness is expected by the time she is a young adult. She is the youngest of two girls in a family in which both parents are also visually impaired. Nancy has always attended regular public schools and is now in second grade. Her parents have encouraged her to live a normal life in every sense of the word. They expect Nancy to be independent and adaptable. She displays these characteristics, as well as optimism and confidence. She talks in an animated way, with considerable fluency. She expresses no self-pity about her disability and views it as a fact of life.

Conclusion

The preceding study of children who cope helps us to balance the frequent negative predictions and expectations made about children at risk from adverse environments or unfavorable endowments. A pathological focus to such phenomena can have negative, self-fulfilling effects by expecting, reinforcing, and maintaining negative trends. This is one of the reasons why early interventions with at-risk children and their families should be done with care and caution.

It is easier to describe the behavior characteristics of children who cope than it is to understand that stress and adversity, instead of being overwhelming, dreaded, and threatening, can be a challenge to overcome. Why some children have this view rather than threat or dread is unknown. The coping child is as equally complex in emotional strengths and normality as the emotionally disturbed or upset child is in weaknesses and pathology.

In the vignettes of children given in this chapter, many complex dynamic factors are observed. In some there are parents who are a source of strength, reinforcers of independence, and models of adaptive behavior. In other examples, the parents are too overwhelmed by their own problems to be helpful, and in still others assistance comes from outside the home. Above-normal intelligence is not a universal characteristic of these children. There may be a nonintellectual type of innate resilience and ability to cope in different individuals, although an equally strong case can be made for resilience acquired through developmental experience. It is also important to recognize that humans are endowed, at least minimally, with the ability to respond to short- and long-term stress through the alarm reaction and the general adaptation response.

It is easier to understand what children do to cope and how they cope, than to know why they do. The assumption, even with the recognition of biologically innate differences, is that their behaviors are learned in complex ways based on different factors for some children than for others. Therefore, it is possible to provide some complex and interesting instructional and therapeutic opportunities for children to learn different behavioral strategies and responses.

It may also be possible to generalize these responses further to real-life situations. These instructional and therapeutic opportunities are called proactive interventions. They should be designed to develop what appear to be the most important and powerful behavioral characteristics of adaptive children. This is why an understanding of coping or stress-resistant children is important. In the next chapter there is a discussion of proactive intervention strategies in general, as well as specific strategies that teachers can use with children in the classroom.

14

Stress-Prevention Strategies

In chapter 13 children who cope with acute and chronic stress were discussed. A number of their behavioral characteristics in feeling, thinking, social, and self domains were described. Given the innate biological determinants that affect behavior, it is assumed that such coping characteristics and competencies are learned and that it might be possible to teach positive, adaptive behavioral strategies to children in classrooms. This type of instruction is referred to as proactive intervention.

Proactive teacher interventions are directed at generating and maintaining coping behavior processes in children in order to foster effective adaptation to difficult life situations and potential future stressful life events of high frequency. They can be considered useful to all children in that stress and unpredictable fates are universal possibilities for all children. These interventions sometimes are referred to as "psychoeducation," which purports to enhance social adjustment, problem-solving abilities, and the general mental health of children. In psychology they are referred to as cognitive behavioral training, since they involve the teaching of behavior.

Distinctions Between Reactive and Proactive Interventions

Distinctions can be made between reactive interventions, which are implemented after a stress event has occured, and proactive interventions, which anticipate or prepare for a possible future stress event. For example, a reactive intervention might involve information and support given to a student about the death of a pet, after the pet was killed. An example of proactive intervention is a fire or tornado drill, which is done in anticipation that such an event might occur. An adequate drill should deal not only with action behaviors but also with the associated feeling and thinking of the pupils.

The distinction between reactive and proactive interventions, however, may not always be so clear. A reactive intervention may eventually result in a positive adaptation to a stress event that may in turn provide a positive basis on which to respond to a stress event in the future. The future event may be of a similar kind or of a different nature. Futhermore, a reactive intervention for one child may have generalized proactive effects on other children in a classroom. For example, talking with a boy about the death of his pet may involve psychological inoculation to the idea of death, for other members of his group or class.

The forms that reactive and proactive teacher interventions take differ somewhat, as shown in table 14.1. Reactive interventions include activities of cognitive understanding, emotional support, structure and control, and skill development. On the other hand, proactive interventions consist of social, cognitive, affective, and self-directed activities. The examples of both types of interventions given in the table illustrate their differences as they pertain to each form involved. Another important difference is that reactive interventions tend to be applied to individual children, while proactive ones often involve the whole group.

The terms *proactive intervention, psychoeducation,* and *cognitive behavioral training* all have similar meanings and shared goals of generating new behaviors that have a positive, adaptive potential for improving the ability to deal with stress events and foster prosocial behaviors. Proactive intervention is a term linked to stress psychology, while psychoeducation is linked to school psychology and cognitive behavior training to behavioralistic psychology.

Psychoeducational Programs

Psychoeducation once was called affective education, in an attempt to apply mental health concepts to school situations and students. Morse and Ravlin's (1979) critical review of the past and current his-

TABLE 14.1 *Comparison of Forms of Reactive and Proactive Teacher*
             Interventions

REACTIVE INTERVENTIONS	
Activity	Example
Cognitive understanding	Connecting stress and behavioral reactions
Emotional expression	Permitting feelings
Emotional support	Showing concern
Structure and control	Modifying school expectations temporarily
Skill development	Analyzing the stress event

PROACTIVE INTERVENTIONS	
Activity	Example
Cognitive style	Fostering means-end thinking
Affective processing	Developing affect tolerance
Social interaction	Understanding the points of view of others
Self-directedness	Generating and maintaining self-esteem

tory of psychoeducation indicates that many programs were overly ambitious, overpromoted, not carefully conceptualized or implemented, and not evaluated. Some public protest developed about schools and teachers involved in these programs, since they seemed to be intruding directly on the values, choices, and emotional life of children. Parents objected because they believed that such private issues were primarily their responsibility. These programs initially achieved popularity under a variety of labels, such as values clarification, emotional education, mental hygiene, affective education, feeling awareness, lifeline, human behavior, human development, self-control, interpersonal skills, transactional analysis, communication skills, sensitivity training, and moral education.

In spite of these criticisms of and unfortunate experiences with affective education, most school professionals and parents would agree that attention to socialization, emotions, attitudes, and values facilitates learning and positive classroom management. Psychoeducation, more broadly defined, can bring together psychology and education, two major streams of professional thought, practice, and experience, based on theoretical concepts, tradition, empirical testing, research, and evaluation. A number of sound programs have evolved from this integration. They can be grouped into two main categories: those that are student focused and those that are teacher focused (Morse & Ravlin, 1979).

A description of some student-focused programs follows:

1. The classroom meeting (Glasser, 1969) involves a teacher-led student group that deals with classroom problems such as caring, individual responsibility, and other topics that can focus on specific problems or be open ended.
2. The "magic circle" (Palomares & Rubini, 1974) is a sequentially structured program for children through sixth grade that teaches about emotions and emphasizes self-awareness, mastery, and social interaction. Children's real-life experiences are the subject matter of the classroom meetings.
3. Self-esteem education (Coopersmith, 1975) emphasizes locus of control and responsibility for one's reactions. Also stressed are self-attributes, expectations of others, and control of feelings.

Some teacher-focused psychoeducational programs are described below:

1. Congruent communication (Ginnott, 1972) suggests that teachers communicate more effectively with children when they address an emotional situation, rationally and without judging a child's character or personality. Objective messages such as teacher ownership and child ownership of feelings rather than subjective blame, criticism, and guilt are taught.
2. Life-space interview (Redl, 1959) is a strategy that works through critical events in the child's classroom life by providing support for emotionally experienced stress (emotional first aid) or by clinical exploration of the nature and meaning of the event (clinical exploration).
3. Logical consequences (Dreikurs & Grey, 1968) is an approach

that avoids teacher punishment or judgment by substituting logical consequences for behaviors. This emphasizes reality, personal responsibility, and acceptable alternatives to maladaptive behavior.

4. Teacher effectiveness training (Gordon, 1974) is based on the identification of problems as student owned or teacher owned. Specific strategies are developed for resolving problems that avoid win or lose confrontations between the teacher and child.

Our appraisal of these programs is that their value to teachers may be more general than specific. They suggest intervention through both teaching content and format strategies and through modifying such teaching practices as overjudging, employing inadequate structure, and not involving students sufficiently in solving their own problems. Difficulties arise or ineffective outcomes result from rigidly applying these programs in overly structured ways. They are more helpful when adapted to the individual styles of teachers and their particular classroom needs. More will be said about this principle after considering other proactive interventions that have been derived from cognitive behavioral psychology and stress psychology.

Cognitive Behavioral Training

Cognitive behavioral psychology has developed from a behaviorist tradition by using cognitive (training or instructional) activities to produce behavioral change through the acquisition of new behaviors and the control and modification of existing behaviors (Kendall & Hollan, 1979). The new behaviors have positive, adaptive, and prosocial characteristics. Methods are employed in which a child thinks about feelings, actions, and problem-solving steps and procedures and may use language as a further facilitator in that process. Sometimes gamelike situations are created using interesting novel materials and procedures to motivate and engage a child's interest. In addition, teacher or therapist modeling is used along with techniques such as role playing, visual imagery, body relaxation, desensitization, coaching, prompting, rehearsing, and talking aloud (verbal mediation). Feedback on performance also may be used, and concrete reinforcements can be added to reward correct performance.

Cognitive behavioral methods have been applied to a wide range of behavioral issues for children and adults. They have been used for symptom modification such as pain regulation, problem drinking, somatic symptoms, smoking, eating disturbances, anxiety, aggressive behavior, and depression. They have been employed in improving body or athletic performance and in fostering academic achievement through developing arithmetic and reading skills or indirectly through improving memory and test-taking abilities. Methods also have been developed for generating prosocial or adaptive behavioral styles. When these are anchored in or based on the actual behavioral characteristics of children and adults who adjust well, then they offer greater potential for validity and effectiveness.

The Psychology of Stress Resistance and Coping

This leads to an examination of two other sources of conceptual support for proactive teacher interventions: stress-resistant children and coping behavioral processes. They have been discussed in previous chapters but are reviewed here since the characteristics of their behavioral processes and outcomes become the goals for proactive interventions. In other words, the goals are to generate the behavioral styles of coping and the behavioral outcome characteristics of stress resistance.

Table 14.2 illustrates the characteristics of stress-resistant children in the four behavioral domains discussed in chapter 13. Is it possible to generate these behaviors through classroom instruction? Behaviors such as empathy, understanding the points of view of others, helping others, good verbal skills, good attentional processes reflectiveness, problem solving, inner locus of control, frustration tolerance, and success appear possible to teach. Other behaviors seem to be more complex and global and do not easily lend themselves to an instructional or training approach. These include the ability to detach from the dysfunctional behaviors of others, being personable and well liked, creative thinking, autonomous thinking, optimism, having a sense of humor, being aware of personal power, having a future orientation, and having a well-developed value system.

In addition to characteristics displayed by stress-resistant children, there are those behavioral processes with which a child responds to

TABLE 14.2   *Behavioral Characteristics of a Stress-Resistant Child, in Social,*
             Cognitive, Affective, and Self Domains

Social

    Personable, well liked by peers and adults

    At ease with people, empathic, understands the points of
    view of others

    Ready to help others in need

    Appropriate classroom behaviors, detaches from dysfunctional
    behaviors of others

    Communicates well with others, good verbal skills

Cognitive

    Autonomous thinking, draws own conclusions

    Good attentional processes, focused and sustained, selective
    skills

    Academically successful, uses information well

    Tests reality, distinguishes fantasy and reality, logical
    thinking

    Reflective, plans behavior, views situations objectively

    Problem solver, means-ends thinking, considers alternatives
    and consequences

    Inner locus of control, accepts responsibility for failure

    Adjusts to novel situations, thinks creatively, uses
    imagination

Affective

    Tolerates frustration and delay in gratification

    Tolerates emotions, can control and express own emotions

    Optimistic

    Sense of humor

Self

    Aware of own power; experiences success

    Positive self-regard; maintains self-esteem

    Resists victimization and negative identity labels

    Future orientation

    Altruistic; well-developed value system

    Has special interests and talents

stress or adversity, particularly the child's approach to stress as a challenge to overcome and master. These processes are listed in table 14.3, once again grouped into social, cognitive, affective, and self behavioral domains. As before, some of these processes appear to be teachable, such as the practice of discussing events with others, flexibility, expressing feelings with control, and acting older than one's actual age. Other characteristics seem less teachable, including having rational perceptions, a creative imagination, being hopeful, being confident, feeling shame when not meeting standards, and having a pull to the future.

In comparing tables 14.2 and 14.3 it can be observed that there are many similarities in the behavioral characteristics grouped in the four domains. This is not entirely surprising. The characteristics listed in table 14.2 come from case and experimental studies of children exposed to chronic environmental and individual stress (Blom, 1984). Those in table 14.3 are derived from the findings of studies of adults who were followed in a long-range longitudinal manner and were considered to be successfully adaptive persons (Haan, 1977). The first group (table 14.2) were in at-risk situations, while the second group (table 14.3) were individuals who stood out positively from the general population.

Using the findings from coping children and adults in the general population and in those exposed to stressful, risky life situations, it is possible to identify a number of adaptive behavior styles for which some proactive interventions have been designed. These interventions can be found in the psychological and psychoeducational literature. More important, teachers may be able to generate their own interventions or to define, clarify, and reinforce prosocial or adaptive behavior styles (processes).

Proactive Programs

There are a number of proactive programs that have been packaged into curriculum materials for use in classrooms. They have been developed for different age or grade groups. Some are rather rigidly structured, while others allow for more flexibility on the part of teachers. These programs usually involve more than one adaptive

TABLE 14.3 *Behavioral Characteristics of Coping Process, in Social, Cognitive, Affective, and Self Domains*

Social

    Discusses upsetting life events with others

    Displays caring and empathy

Cognitive

    Has reasonable, realistic perceptions

    Exercises creative imagination

    Ability to concentrate

    Displays purposeful behavior

    Has problem-solving approach

    Demonstrates flexibility, considers alternative choices

    Internal locus of control

    Considers consequences

    Seeks out information

Affective

    Expresses feelings with control

    Feels shame when standards are not met

    Hopefulness

Self

    Tries to master and overcome

    Acts older than actual age

    Has high frustration tolerance

    Persistence

    Is oriented to present needs

    Feels pull to future

    Feels self-confidence

Source: Haan, 1977.

style, since these behaviors are not independent of one another. The behavioral dimensions, listed in table 14.4, overlap with one another. For example, while the "Listening" program of Cooke and Parsons (1963) is directed at auditory attention skills, it also involves reflective style, internalization, and problem solving. Another program, the "Turtle Technique" (Schneider & Robin, 1973, 1976) generates inhibition of impulsive, acting-out, and aggressive behavior through visual imagery. "Think Aloud" makes use of verbal mediation (language or private speech) in guiding cognitive and emotional problem solving (Camp & Bash, 1981).

In the following sections, we present reviews done by Spivack, Platt, and Shure (1976) of two programs that deal with social cognition and problem solving.

Listening

A program called "Listening" (Cooke & Parsons, 1963) is described in some detail since it is easily applied to regular and special education classrooms. This intervention has a number of goals: (1) to take a reflective stance toward problem-solving activities, (2) to de-

TABLE 14.4 *Adaptive Behavioral Styles on Which to Base Proactive Interventions*

Affective expression concerns the mobilization and control of various feeling states such as anger, arousal, and anxiety.

Attentional processes deal with various cognitive attributes such as focusing attention in auditory and visual modes, scanning, sustained as well as selective attention, and shifts in thinking sets.

Internalization consists of gratification delay, affect tolerance, following rules, not externalizing or acting out feelings, and keeping feelings available yet within the person.

Locus of control involves self control and responding to events in a discriminating fashion, as either within one's own control and responsibility (internal locus) or resulting from external situations and other persons (external locus).

Problem solving concerns task analysis, planning ahead, means-ends thinking, awareness of consequences, flexible approaches, and alternative solutions.

Reflective styles consist of delay in responding, monitoring happenings, appraising situations and thinking before acting.

Social cognition involves empathy, altruism, decentering, perception of the reactions of others, awareness of social situations, and taking the role of others.

velop and use focal auditory attention, (3) to break down complex auditory information into simpler elements and analyze their characteristics, and (4) to synthesize auditory elements into an organized, meaningful response.

A gamelike situation is created for groups of six to ten children, lasting thirty to forty minutes. The activity is to be done twice a week for an extended period of time. Children usually find the activities challenging, interesting, and fun. The teacher can easily generate auditory information that provides an opportunity for imaginativeness, by developing recordings of simple sounds, sound sequences, and sound situations.

There are three levels of sound games that can be played. The first level consists of single sounds of objects, starting with simple, familiar sounds (horn, bell, hammer striking) and proceeding to more complex, less familiar sounds (sound of a light switch or a bat meeting a ball). The goal is to identify the object making the sound. The second level consists of sequences of sounds associated with activities, starting with easy, familiar sequences (making toast, buttering it, and putting jam on it) to more difficult, less familiar sequences (putting paper in a typewriter, typing, taking the paper out). The goal is to determine the activity and its sequences. The third level consists of the many sounds that come from complex situations, such as an automobile service station, an airport, or a barber shop. The goal is to identify the source of the sounds and the situations in which they are located. The teacher determines the level to be played according to the age of the children and their previous experience. It may be helpful with older children to run through the first two levels quickly, for practice.

In playing the sound games the teacher needs to stress processes, procedures, clues, thinking, asking questions, and reflecting; guessing and impulsive answers must be discouraged. The teacher may want to refer to playing detective, in which there is searching and thinking about clues. When students follow the guidelines, the teacher praises and encourages them. There are also three basic questions that children learn to ask in the game:

1. What kind of material(s) make(s) a sound like that?
2. What kinds of objects are made of this material?
3. Which of these objects is most likely to make the sound?

Cooke and Parsons (1963) report that this procedure, used over a period of a year with severely emotionally disturbed children, appeared to have a number of beneficial effects. These included excitement and interest in the materials and methods used, identification with the model of the detective, pride in thoughtful questions, greater use of imagination, careful exploration of details, shift from impulsive guessing to reflective questioning, and more importance placed on good questions. Their clinical impressions were that these adaptive behaviors generalized from the listening class to the school program at large.

"Think Aloud"

The assessment of the effectiveness of this proactive intervention program went beyond clinical evaluation, by using standardized behavior checklist scales as pretest and posttest measures (Camp, Blom, Hebert & van Doorninck, 1977). This program is named "Think Aloud" because it utilizes verbal mediation techniques in cognitive and emotional problem-solving activities. It was originally designed to improve self-control in certain early elementary schoolboys who were impulsive and aggressive, and it proved to be effective in modifying these behaviors.

"Think Aloud" was expanded to involve the use of modeling and verbalized thinking in dealing with cognitive and interpersonal problems. This type of oral thinking is called *verbal mediation*, indicating that language can be a regulator of thought and feeling. Verbal mediation occurs naturally in children and adults engaged in problem solving, but it may not be recognized as a constructive strategy by teachers in the classroom. In "Think Aloud," children are deliberately trained to talk to themselves in effective and skillful ways by modeling teacher behaviors and practicing these same behaviors alone. The approach is applied to structured, cognitive-problem activities and social-problem situations presented in pictures. In the latter situations children are trained to verbalize problem identification, plans, solutions, and consequences.

The published "Think Aloud" program (Camp & Bash, 1981) consists of twenty-three lesson plans for daily half-hour sessions over a period of ten weeks with some lessons taking several sessions to complete and children progressing at their own rates. The teaching manual is designed so that it can be used easily by the classroom teacher. Usually the program is applied to individual children or children in pairs, in which case the instructor would have to be a resource teacher or special child-support staff member (psychologist, counselor, nurse, or social worker). However, the program can also be used in groups of up to four. Some adaptations can also be made for use in a larger classroom.

A list of some of the lesson plans includes the following:

Copy Cat Game (Simon Says)
Alternative Plans
Labeling
Causality and Categorization
Think Aloud Quietly
Generating Solutions
Predicting Consequences
Auditory Inhibition
Evaluating by Fairness
Evaluating by Effectiveness
Evaluating Solutions

A manual is provided that details the materials and procedures to be used. Students model a teacher's actions and verbal statements.

Conclusion

Proactive teacher interventions lack systemization and represent an area of developing knowledge and experience. Many interventions remain experimental and have not been adapted for classroom use. Others have not been sufficiently evaluated. It has been difficult to demonstrate whether benefits occur or are maintained and whether they generalize to situations beyond the specific intervention. However, a few programs from psychoeducation, cognitive behavioral training, and stress psychology sources have been useful to classroom teachers. A larger number are valuable in providing teachers with strategies and techniques they can adapt for their own use. While proactive intervention is a field where much developmental, implementation, and evaluation work remains to be done, its goal is to develop a systematic approach where the teacher can (1) select a behavioral characteristic to generate, (2) find a feasible and effective program for generating the behavior, and (3) apply the program to a class or subset of a class.

15

Children's Literature in Stress and Coping

Children's literature provides a special medium for reactive intervention in children's stress. It is a form of material many teachers feel comfortable using in the classroom since it involves a familiar class activity of reading, listening to, and analyzing a story. When used in stress intervention, the story selected has as its theme a particular stressor, and the procedure consists of encouraging children to react, through discussion, to the story elements and the characters' behavioral reactions. However, the cognitive and language skills of reading, listening, speaking, and analysis are employed, just as in other familiar language learning activities. The use of children's literature as a reactive intervention can be used with a single child, with a small group of children, or with an entire class, with minor variations in procedure. This makes it possible to process the same stressor in the lives of a number of children, to sensitize other children to the feelings of children experiencing stress, and to engage in problem solving around possible future stressors. In the latter, a reactive intervention strategy can become proactive for some children.

Influence of Story Content on Children's Behavior

Studies of the content of stories in basal readings textbooks and trade books have focused on their instrumental, motivational, socializing, and behavioral influences on children in the educational setting (Blom, 1978). Another stream of professional experience has also developed from a therapeutic emphasis in which the content or theme of a story not only is a source of information but also has a positive emotional impact on the reader. This concept has been referred to as bibliotherapy, connoting that books can produce various helpful direct psychological effects (Riggs, 1978). A third area that contributes to an understanding of the content of books is the study of reading processes from affective and cognitive perspectives (Blom, 1979).

From these sources of information and experiences, it can be conceptualized that reading often serves multiple psychological purposes. These include fantasy expression and gratification, channeling impulsive expression, providing information that aids reality testing, offering ideas and values that can guide behavior, dealing with universal conflicts and feelings, nurturing cognitive development and functioning, substituting thought for motor action, liberating oneself from one's own environment, offering comic relief, finding pleasure in words and ideas, and preparing for and integrating life experiences. Children can experience these feelings and thoughts if they are given enough favorable opportunities with appropriate literature and with adequate processing opportunities.

The selection of books aimed at achieving these ends offers both challenges and opportunities for teachers. There are many books that deal with such childhood issues of family life, children's emotions, biological events, and stressful happenings. They vary in quality from the very poorly conceived and written, which tend to be Pollyannaish presentations, to stories with an engaging and convincing plot, including books that are considered literary efforts.

A number of positive consequences may occur when a child reads a story with a pertinent psychological theme. First, the child may realize that she or he is not the only one experiencing problems. Recognizing similarities between oneself and fictional characters may lead to better understanding of situations and even suggest solutions. A chance to discuss the story with an understanding teacher may be of help to the child. Through an understanding of the character in a story, the child may develop a better understanding of himself or herself. Identification may go beyond personal characterization to include others in the story and the child's own life. Second, a child who identifies with a fictional character may imitate that character. When the real persons in the child's life do not provide appropriate models, fictional characters may. Third, an important advantage to reading as a form of intervention is that the child is in control. He or she can choose not to continue, or to continue at a pace appropriate to his or her feelings.

Counseling Children Through Stories

Individual counseling experiences we have had with children point to ways in which stories and the characters in them represent important identifications, prototypes of good and evil, and conflict resolution. Let us consider some case examples.

• Karen, age fifteen, was admitted to the hospital for the study of possible endocrine gland disease. Both Karen and her mother seized on this suggestion as the possible explanation for long-standing problems in their relationship. Karen did poorly in school, had few friends, had adenoid speech, complained of abdominal pain, and periodically soiled her undergarments. She was somewhat unkempt and did not care about her dress and physical appearance. In contrast, her mother was immaculately and stylishly dressed and quite attractive.

Karen, in her isolation, wrote fictional stories at home which she was reluctant to share at first. In addition, she read a good deal and was more willing to discuss some of these books. In spite of doing poor academic work in school, she was reading Shakespeare's *Merchant of Venice*. When asked what she thought of this book, she recited a passage by Shylock in a very poignant manner: "I am a Jew. Hath not a Jew eyes? hath not a Jew hands, organs, dimensions, senses, affections, passions? . . . If you prick us, do we not bleed? if you tickle us, do we not laugh? if you poison us, do we not die? and if you wrong us, shall we not revenge?" (Act III, Scene i).

It seemed that Karen's low self-esteem, the plea for acceptance, the feelings of rejection, her somewhat persecuted view of the world, and her pent-up resentment and revenge were portrayed in Shylock's speech. It took some time before these views and feelings about herself could be understood and processed more directly in a counseling relationship.

• Harry was a bright nine-year-old boy who was aggressive and impulsive, the worst kid on the bus, and constantly disruptive at school and at home. He was in counseling treatment for quite a long time. When his behavior improved a little, he became interested in going to

Hebrew school on Saturday mornings. From this source, he learned a good deal about old Hebrew stories and in his counseling sessions began to play out themes that dealt with rivalry, hatred, and expected retaliation from others. For a number of sessions Harry's play centered on Absalom and his father, David. Absalom was a rivalrous son who wanted to destroy or appropriate his father's power and possessions. His fate of being hung by his hair was the frightening consequence of such overpowering ambitions and wishes.

Shylock and Absalom are classic characters from old stories, but children are drawn to characters in modern literature as well.

• Tim, a fourteen-year-old physically disabled boy in a special education program, was enamored of Long John Silver, the fictional character in *Treasure Island* (Stevenson, 1915). Long John had a peg leg, a threatening cutlass, and a patched eye, and was the purveyor of the black spot curse. This character synthesized a number of important identification elements for Tim: his views and feelings about having a genetic neuromuscular disease (a black spot curse), wearing half casts on his lower legs so that he could walk (peg legs), and physically and verbally threatening and intimidating other children and adults (brandishing a cutlass).

• John Wilkes Booth of historical infamy represented for eight-year-old Saul his aggressive feelings toward a too-kindly, overly permissive father and the boy's expectation that his feelings would result in a retaliatory fate of pursuit, capture, inquiry, trial, and death. In a number of sessions, Saul would climb on the play table while the therapist was sitting. When the therapist wasn't looking, Saul would jump on the therapist's back, yelling, "John Wilkes Booth!" He then would dash out of the room and down the hall, with the therapist in pursuit. He was caught and then an inquiry followed back in the office.

Children can also write their own stories in therapy, and some particularly enjoy the activity as a way of expressing their wishes, conflicts, and anxieties. The results would hardly be classified as literature, although there are a few exceptions to that. A variety of short stories and longer productions have emerged under such names as *Silly Looks* (about a boy with facial tics), *Vinny da Bum and His Family* (about a boy with very aggressive behavior), *1001 Horrible Recipes* (a very long production about a boy with fears about body intactness and disturbances in body functions), *A Dictionary of Forbidden Words* (about an inhibited, phobic boy), and *Gardo Pack* (another one about a boy who was very aggressive). Writing offers many possibilities to children: It can be a way to express personal issues in a disguised form, to use language rather than body and physical action, to obtain clarification and interpretation about their problems, and to provide solutions to various conflicts through negotiation. In the process, children seem to gain a cognitive language competence that is facilitated by their dealing with content of personal relevance and importance. In the example of Vinny da Bum, it was possible to terminate aggressive behavior through a story that eventually had to have an ending.

Teacher's Guides to Children's Literature

Teachers may select books that focus on particular stress events and encourage a child or children to react to the content of the book. A number of reference books are available for that purpose.

One index, *The Book Finder* (Dreyer, 1977), contains annotations of 1,031 children's books published before 1975. These annotations are organized according to topics that are often stressful to children, ranging from abandonment and abortion through childhood worries and being the youngest child. This is perhaps the largest single source of children's titles organized around stress events and will prove invaluable for a teacher searching for such books. The International Youth Library (1982) has compiled a bibliography of books for handicapped children about various physical and mental impairments.

A guide to the use of such books, which also provides critiques of their content as well as suggestions on how to use them with children, is *Helping Children Cope* (Fassler, 1978). The author combines an understanding of child behavior with a knowledge and appreciation of children's literature. Her book includes topics such as death, forms of separation, bedtime fears, school experiences, separation from family and friends, hospitalization and illness, birth of a sibling, moving, adoption, divorce, family financial stress, parent unemployment, imprisonment of a family member, natural disasters, and emergencies. For each topic, Fassler presents a psychological discussion followed by possible reactions children may have and a listing of books with related themes. She illustrates how children's stories can be helpful in encouraging discussions about sensitive psychological issues. These stories also help parents, teachers, and other adults introduce such issues to children when they are difficult for the adults as well.

Fassler's recommendations for books related to specific topics include the following:[1]

> *The Tenth Good Thing About Barney* (Viorst, 1971)—about death
> *Shawn Goes to School* (Brienburg, 1973)—about separation
> *Madeline* (Bemelmans, 1939)—about illness and hospitalization
> *She Come Bringing Me That Little Baby Girl* (Greenfield, 1974)—
>   about the birth of a sibling
> *The New Boy on the Sidewalk* (Craig, 1967)—about moving
> *I Am Adopted* (Lapsley, 1974)—about adoption
> *A Month of Sundays* (Blue, 1972)—about divorce
> *Firestorm* (Gee, 1968)—about natural disasters and emergencies

Cianciolo (1975) describes how "feeling books" for children help develop their social and personal sensitivities. By "feeling books" she refers to earthy, vital, alive, and realistic writing that engages the reader in the story. She describes how the child reader experiences various feelings and emotions and identifies with different human events. Cianciolo cites a number of examples of children's literature, such as *Julie of the Wolves* (George, 1972), which presents themes of running away, isolation, and hunger; *The Bears' House* (Sachs, 1971), about an unhappy girl from a fatherless home with a depressed mother; *Sue Ellen* (Hunter, 1969), which portrays a girl who is failing in school and comes from an economically poor family; and *The Greyhound* (Griffiths, 1966), about conflict between a boy and his parents over having to give up a beloved pet.

Gardner (1971, 1973) has written stories to be read to children by adults, covering the subjects of divorce, one-parent families, and minimal brain dysfunction. These stories provide the opportunity for

---

[1]Complete reference information for the children's books cited in the rest of this chapter can be found in the list at the end of the chapter.

children to discuss these events and experiences as they personally affect them.

There are also other sources of information about children's books that are written around themes involving children in specific stressful situations. *Books That Help Children Deal with a Hospital Experience,* prepared by the U.S. Department of Health, Education and Welfare (1974), is an excellent reference in that it includes titles of both current and out-of-print books, indications of age-level appropriateness of books, and a publisher's index. Books for children, teenagers, and adults, as well as selected audiovisual materials, are recommended by Schwartz (1977), for those involved in "death education."

In working with both children and teachers, we have identified books for children on other topics that are potentially stressful for children. A number of these books are included in the list of Children's Book References at the end of this chapter.

Teacher Interventions
Using Children's Literature

An example of how teachers might use children's literature as a reactive intervention is described by an elementary teacher (Ingall, 1983). She reported on the use of books for helping children in the stress of divorce. Two students in her third-grade class had parents who were going through divorce. Ingall was also aware of three other students whose parents were already divorced and one girl whose mother had died when the girl was age five. These students from time to time would talk with Ingall about their feelings and problems in their family situations. Through a discussion with the school social worker about the problems these children were having, it was decided to teach a unit on the family to the whole class, using books to provide the focus and structure in dealing with the stressors of divorce and death.

In implementing the unit, four sessions were organized for consecutive Monday afternoons during the last part of the school day, from 2:30 to 3:15 P.M. The teacher and school social worker taught them as a team. One read a story and the other followed with an activity that processed the feelings and reactions of the children.

In the first session, the book *All Kinds of Families* (Simon, 1976) was read to the class. Each student was given a large sheet of white paper and instructed to draw her or his own family. After the pictures were drawn, the students were encouraged to show their pictures and to talk about them. Almost every child wanted to do this show-and-tell activity, but there was insufficient time for everyone to do so. At the beginnning of the drawing time, some children asked questions about the "right" way to do the picture. The instructions to "draw the picture any way you want" were repeated, encouraging the children to include anyone they wanted in the pictures.

All Kinds of Families is a book about a variety of family forms, including families from different ethnic groups, three-generational families, single-parent families, adopted families, small and large families, extended families with a variety of relatives living in the same home, and unrelated people living together as a family. The presentation is positive and supportive about different family forms and deals realistically with feelings, such as anger and sadness, that occur within the different family frameworks.

In the second session *A New Mother for Martha* (Green, 1978) was read to the class, followed by a group discussion of the events in the book and feelings about those events. In the third and fourth sessions, *Boys and Girls Book about Divorce* (Gardner, 1971) was read. The students were eager and some even anxious to share personal experiences and feelings. The girl whose mother had died when she was young talked about that and her father's new lady friend. Several other children talked about deaths of family members and their feelings about those deaths. The discussions were not limited to divorced and reconstituted families. Students welcomed the opportunity to talk about death, divorce, and other frightening events that had occurred to them or others.

This teaching unit on the family was developed out of a recognized need to help a number of children who were experiencing stress from divorce and death. It was an intervention that was both proactive and reactive. It was proactive in generating coping, increased awareness, and adaptive behavior that any of the students might use in the future with events surrounding separation, divorce, or death in their own families. Specifically, these interventions involved opportunities for the children to practice reflective thinking, problem solving, internalized responses, and consideration of alternative solutions. The teacher and school social worker also provided modeling in that they

they showed confidence in dealing with upsetting events and potential future events.

The teaching unit was a reactive intervention in providing structure and organization for those children who were expressing anxiety and concern over divorce and death events. It also taught behaviors such as directing attention, showing concern, using physical activity, recognizing peer support, listening, labeling, clarifying, supporting, acknowledging, and praising. This unit is presented here, not because another teacher might use it exactly as described, but because it illustrates the kind of interventions that teachers can develop, with children's literature as the medium.

Children's Book References

Bemelmans, L. (1939). *Madeline*. New York: Viking Press. (Hospitalization)

Blue, R. (1972). *A month of Sundays*. New York: Franklin Watts. (Parental separation)

Blue, R. (1972). *Grandma didn't wave back*. New York: Franklin Watts. (Aging)

Brienburg, D. (1973). *Shawn goes to school*. Illus. by E. Lloyd. New York: Thomas Crowell. (Starting school)

Buck, P. (1966). *Matthew, Mark, Luke and John*. New York: John Day. (Abandonment, stealing)

Craig, J. (1967). *The new boy on the sidewalk*. Illus. by S. Greenwald. New York: W.W. Norton. (Family move)

Cunningham, J. (1970). *Burnish me bright*. New York: Pantheon. (Speech impairment)

DuBois, W. (1969). *Porko von Popbutton*. New York: Harper & Row. (Overweight)

Fassler, J. (1978). *Howie helps himself*. Chicago: Albert Whitman. (Physical handicap)

Gardner, R. (1971). *Boys and girls book about divorce*. New York: Science House.

Gardner, R. (1973). *The family book about minimal brain dysfunction*. New York: Aronson.

Gee, M. (1968). *Firestorm*. New York: William Morrow. (Experience in a fire)

George, J. (1972). *Julie of the wolves*. Illus. by J. Schoenherr. New York: Harper & Row. (Isolation, running away)

Green, P. (1978). *A new mother for Martha*. Illus. by J. Lasker. New York: Human Sciences Press. (Stepparent)

Greenfield, E. (1974). *She come bringing me that little baby girl*. Illus. by J. Steptoe. Philadelphia: Lippincott. (New baby sister)

Griffiths, H. (1966). *The greyhound*. Illus. by V. Ambrus. New York: Doubleday. (Parent/child conflict)

Hunter, E. (1969). *Sue Ellen*. Illus. by B. Holmes. Boston: Houghton Mifflin. (Retardation)

Keats, E. (1969). *Goggles*. New York: Macmillan. (Bullying)

Kingman, L. (1970). *The Peter Pan bag*. Boston: Houghton Mifflin. (Drug problems)

Lapsley, S. (1974). *I am adopted*. Illus. by M. Charlton. Scarsdale, NY: Bradbury Press. (Adoption)

Sachs, M. (1971). *The bears' house*. Illus. by L. Glanzman. Garden City, NY: Doubleday. (Mentally ill parent)

Seixas, J. (1979). *Living with a parent who drinks too much*. New York: William Morrow. (Problem drinking parent)

Simon, N. (1976). *All kinds of families*. Illus. by J. Lasker. Chicago: Albert Whitman. (Different family forms)

Stanek. M. (1970). *Tall Tina*. Chicago: Albert Whitman. (Physical differences)

Terris, S. (1972). *On fire*. Garden City, NY Doubleday. (Peer relations)

Viorst, J. (1971). *The tenth good thing about Barney*. Illus. by E. Blequad. New York: Atheneum Press. (Death of a pet)

16

Using the Stress-Intervention Model

The first nine chapters of this book describe a model of teacher-directed intervention in stress events and situations in children's lives, along with suggestions for implementing the model in elementary classrooms. Throughout these chapters the traditional role of the teacher is maintained, so the skills and understanding required to implement the intervention strategies are consistent with the concept of the teacher as a helping professional.

Chapters 10, 11, and 12 describe common stressors in the lives of children; these are associated with family, health, and schooling. Teachers come in contact with these stress events and situations on a regular basis, so the information about them is designed to clarify and explain phenomena already familiar to teachers.

Chapter 13, on children who cope, reminds teachers that the response to stress need not be negative and the results need not be maladaptive. Most children respond adaptively to stress, and many are challenged by modest levels of stress. The stress-intervention model addresses the minority of the instances where responses to stress are pathological and maladaptive.

For those teachers who want to take a more preventive approach to stress in children, chapter 14 on proactive interventions offers a brief introduction to the area of psychosocial education.

Children's literature as a specific form of both reactive and proactive intervention is presented in chapter 15. Since children's literature is familiar to teachers, they should be comfortable using it as an intervention in children's stress.

This final chapter sets forth a number of considerations for implementing the model, as well as some cautions and limitations.

Teacher Concerns About Responding to Stress in Children

While teachers are prepared to deal with groups of children rather than individual children, the stress-intervention model suggests steps and procedures to follow in helping individuals. It is not expected that teachers should be therapists, but they can be therapeutic by helping, ameliorating, and improving. At times a life event or chronic situation for a child may cause discomfort for a teacher, particularly when trying to help a child deal with it. A teacher can be uncomfortable and yet be helpful. Identifying and processing stress in children may make a teacher, or for that matter any helping professional, feel uneasy at times. With practice and experience this diminishes.

Teachers may experience discomfort in relation to particular stressors such as abuse, rape, death of a parent, or alcoholism in the family. In a case discussed earlier in this book, a student teacher experienced distress during show-and-tell when a six-year-old boy exposed his back to reveal welts and bruises made by a belt. She interrupted his presentation and told him she would talk with him later. She knew that the event had to be discussed with the boy, but she gave herself time to collect her nerves and to talk it over with a respected colleague. The next day, after talking individually with the boy, she discussed what had happened with the class and gave the children a chance to tell how they felt.

At times it can be reassuring to a child to have a teacher share feelings about an event in the child's life. The teacher should act as a model, by expressing feelings without displaying excessive emotion. A child may be comforted by knowing that he or she is not alone in discomfort.

Sometimes teachers are concerned that they may cause psychological "hurt" to a child by intervening without the knowledge of a behavioral expert. This concern is not justified. If a teacher displays tact, a wish to be helpful, empathy, and concern for a child experiencing stress, there is little danger of being harmful, even if the intervention tactic is ineffective. Inaction may be in greater error at times than the risk of an improper action. To show empathy for a child will be therapeutic. Recalling one's own life as a child may help a teacher be empathic. This may be done privately and shared tactfully with a child.

Applying the model of stress intervention fits into normal classroom activity for teachers. While time is involved, it should be a reasonable amount with positive payoffs for the classroom atmosphere and learning environment. Sensitive teachers have used many of the interventions described in the previous chapters for many years. Some of the group interventions involve only slight alterations of standard teaching procedures and may accomplish emotional as well as cognitive learning. For example, when the classroom activity is reading aloud, a story can be selected with content that is relevant to stress and coping. The goal is to systematize and provide a rationale for teacher interventions with children who experience stress in their lives. This means going beyond intuitive thinking and action by using a model for stress intervention to guide and focus more thoughtful actions.

Some teachers may have concerns or questions about their roles in helping children with stress or in generating coping and prosocial behaviors. These concerns focus on three areas: (1) the personal level and (2) the interactional level involving children and parents, and (3) the organizational level, involving colleagues, advisors, and school administrators.

The Personal Level

At the personal level it seems natural for a teacher to be an advocate for a child by improving conditions and the adjustments of children, thus enabling them to be more effective in coping with stressors. It is important to remember that children spend one-third of their waking lives in school and that five hours a day, five days a week can constitute a great deal of impact time. There are no other human service professionals who have this frequent and prolonged contact with children. Like other professionals who work with children, teachers may overidentify with them, lose their realistic perspective, and try to be more influential than their parents. It should also be recognized that a child may distort, misinterpret, or overidealize a teacher's actions or statements. This may be taken home to parents, causing them to become upset and even resentful. If such problems arise among the child, parents, and teacher, they can almost always be resolved if the teacher does not become defensive and react negatively. With good intentions, clarification, and problem-solving skills, misunderstandings are almost always resolved, and are sometimes followed by successful resolution of a problem. There are, of course, a few situations where misunderstanding and conflict remain; in such cases the problem may require the assistance of other professional people.

The Interactional Level

There is also an interactional level of concern for teachers. One aspect of this concern is how to foster an interaction with children such that stress events can be discussed. Classroom experiences indicate that, if teachers let children know they are interested in their lives and problems, children will turn to them. There is a strong possibility of being swamped by requests for individual talks. It is a question of management—selecting the important stress events, deciding on how much time to allot, and including activities at sensible times during the day. While the expectation is that children will talk, it is also important to give them space and the option not to share or involve the teacher if they do not wish to do so.

Sometimes teachers are concerned about the reactions and feelings of parents, concerning their classroom interventions. Should parents be informed ahead of time about the teacher's role and functions, including the management of stress and coping? Should they be informed about specific reactive and proactive interventions before or after the fact? Should these activities be considered a part of usual classroom teaching? There are no absolute answers to such questions. They involve the judgment of the teacher. The teacher should not feel that all interventions must be disclosed to parents for approval. There is no need either to avoid or inflame. When a parent is informed, language that is neither threatening nor alarming should be used to describe what is being done. Anything a teacher does that has the power to influence or change behavior involves some element of risk. If difficulties arise, the teacher should not become defensive and guilt ridden, but believe in the basic assumption that what is being done is helpful to children (therapeutic). Most difficulties can be resolved through listening, clarification, and explanation. Relationships between teachers and parents can be strengthened in the process. Parents may confuse reactive and proactive interventions with sensitivity training or values clarification procedures, and this may cause concern. The approach described in this book will usually involve a fair amount of parent contact, which is apt to gain their approval and support.

The Organizational Level

A final area of teacher concern is at the organizational level, which involves colleagues, advisors, and administrators. When working with children, it is important to share one's experiences with school professionals who can be trusted. Some advisors and administrators are overly cautious and conservative. They may follow the old adage, "If you sleep on the floor, you can't fall out of bed." It may not be advisable or necessary to share what is being done with them. Again, teacher judgment is involved in what to communicate. The teacher should follow the same guidelines as stated previously: (1) believe in the basic idea of helping children who are under stress, (2) do not feel defensive or guilty, and (3) explain and clarify what is being done should questions arise. It can be generally assumed that school people share the same goals of helping children.

Parental Acceptance of Teacher Interventions

Experience, common sense, and educational and communications theories all support the notion that children are well served when their teachers are in regular communication with their parents. When the important adults in a child's life share common concerns for moral and intellectual development, the child is given an enormous advantage. Even when these adults are in less than total agreement, there are advantages for the child who knows that they are all his or her advocates.

Parents sometimes have a rather conservative view of the purposes of schooling. Often this view does not include teacher involvement in nonacademic matters of socialization or moral or self-concept development. Probably most parents would admit that there are a certain number of such activities that will inevitably occur, but some would prefer that teachers take no intentional measures to promote personal development in nonacademic areas. The number of parents who have such conservative views about schooling may be small in relation to the total population of parents, but it is common for those of this persuasion to be fairly vocal about their belief that the school ought to confine its attention to traditional academic pursuits.

Many educators agree that the social, moral, and intellectual aspects of the development of children are so inextricably combined that it is unrealistic to focus attention on one aspect only. It is the whole child who stands before the teacher to be educated. Failure to notice and react to the stresses that the child is experiencing is tantamount to a failure to provide even the academic fare that is the priority of many.

The stress-intervention model that is described in this book might convey a wrong impression in the minds of some parents who would hear about it without enough information to understand its purpose fully. The model is intended to facilitate the accomplishment of normal teaching responsibilities, and it is not a radical departure from or extension of traditional teaching activities. Applying the model does not require teachers to engage in therapy, probe the psychological recesses of the mind, or intrude upon the legitimate privacy of the family. It merely provides a systematic way of thinking about the behavioral changes that are commonly observed by teachers, and it suggests that teachers can respond to these behavioral changes in appropriate and helpful ways. Parents and teachers who understand the model will see it as a plan for improving the services that teachers have always wished to provide for children but have often found too awesome to deal with. Use of the model may invigorate teachers by calling attention to the substantial number of children who are quite effective in dealing with stress and to those few remarkable children who seem to rise above the chronically stressful environments in which they live. Application of the model should also provide concrete suggestions for reactive intervention, as well as encourage teachers to intervene in ways that will not trample on the sensibilities of parents.

In communicating with parents it is important to avoid the use of technical terms that suggest psychological conditions or diagnoses that are inappropriate for teachers to assign. Even the use of the "stress-intervention model" as a descriptor might appear to formalize or extend the role of the teacher beyond what is acceptable to some parents. Expressing interest in and concern for children is apt to enlist the friendship and cooperation of parents. Discussing ways of dealing with behaviors that have been observed in school may provide ideas that parents will accept and use at home. Conversing with parents in depth about their children will surface useful information and may even teach parents, by implication, some needed child-rearing skills. Parents who lack skills and knowledge and who find an educated ally in their efforts to provide a supportive home for their children are not very likely to become adversaries. The line that may be thought of as separating "meddling" from legitimate concern is probably a fine one, and its proper placement may vary with one's assessment of each set of parents. Teachers, experienced in human relationships as they are, have traditionally been quite sensitive in judging how best to deal with different parents. That skill, however it is acquired, will need continued application.

Stress Intervention and Stress Management

A distinction must be made here between stress intervention and stress management. While stress intervention has been the focus of this book, there are a number of human service professionals who advocate teaching children one or more stress-management techniques (Schultz, 1980; Springer, 1983). The stress-management viewpoint has a quantitative but nonspecific aspect; that is, it is the amount or level of stress, rather than specific stressful events, that has particular psychological meaning (Freese, 1979). It focuses on the physiological response aspect of stress rather than on the stimulus event in the environment, and it emphasizes body fitness and control, lifestyle concerns, and general psychobiological measures, all of which can be addressed in anticipation of stress occurring in peoples' lives (Adams, 1978). A wide variety of management techniques have been tried and recommended for adults and children, especially in groups. Some of these are relaxation, exercise, positive mental attitude, cognitive understanding, recreation, general fitness, biofeedback, meditation and concentration, catharsis, group discussion, social support, assertiveness, effective planning, stress awareness, and good nutrition (Germeroth, 1978; Meichenbaum, 1976; Rossman & Kohrweiler, 1977).

Stress intervention, however, as described in this book, involves identifying the qualitative features of stress, including the psychological aspects of the stimulus event. More attention is given to the mental aspects of stress, the nature of behavioral responses, and how responses are processed for a given individual. Interventions, for the most part, are directed at individuals and focus on those aspects most likely to be beneficial, such as the stress itself, behavioral reactions, and behavioral processes. Distinctions are made between reactive interventions, which occur after a stress event has happened, and proactive interventions, which are used in anticipation of stress or in generating prosocial adaptive behavior styles.

We make no attempt to critique the stress-management approach. The focus here is on stress intervention, which holds the most promise for classroom teachers and children.

Stress Intervention and Classroom Management

Some teachers are eager to improve their classroom management techniques, and occasionally view the stress-intervention model as a system of classroom management. It is not intended as such and probably will do little to assist a teacher in need of better management techniques. However, to the extent that stress leads to maladaptive behaviors in children that create problems in the classroom, the model may be of some help in reducing classroom disorder.

Once a teacher becomes familiar with the stress-intervention model, there may be a tendency to assume that stress is the cause of all the unacceptable classroom behavior of children. Clearly, stress is not the cause of all impulsive and aggressive behavior. Application of the stress-intervention model is more apt to succeed in those situations in which a known stress event or condition occurs or when an obvious change in behavior suggests a need to look for an unknown stressor. Interventions that are implemented in the absence of a known stressor are far less likely to succeed.

Limits to the Stress-Intervention Model

The stress-intervention model is not applicable to all the problems of the elementary classroom. If the limitations of this model are not kept in mind and observed by the teacher, and if attempts are made to apply it to situations for which it is not appropriate, disillusionment with it is sure to occur.

The model is not often applicable to groups of children. Stressors usually occur to individuals rather than to entire groups, such as a class or an entire school population. Certainly the responses to stressors are different, so that an appropriate intervention strategy for any given child at a specific point in time is likely not to be appropriate to many other children in the class at that same time. Even in the instance of a group stressor, the reactions of the children involved are usually so individualized that group interventions are neither practical to implement nor likely to be effective for most members of the group. So while many of the proactive intervention strategies suggested in chapter 14 are applicable to groups, the reactive strategies suggested by the intervention model usually are appropriate only for individual children.

As discussed earlier, one early step in applying the model is the identification of a single stress event or condition. Often this single stressor will be embedded in a myriad of stressors, anxieties, and reactions that may in turn become stressors, so that identification can be a difficult problem. For the emotionally disturbed or impaired child, this step of stressor identification is extremely important and also much more difficult. The difficulty involved in stressor identification in emotionally disturbed children makes this model less likely to succeed with them. However, it may be useful for any child when a stressor can be identified and dealt with. This may allow the child to concentrate on the other stressors involved and also reduce the cumulative effect of multiple stressors.

With the many demands placed upon the teacher, including the self-imposed ones, and the conflicts that invariably arise between teacher and students, it is inevitable that at some point the teacher will want to say, "I've had it with this kid." What happens next? It is probable that the relationship will not end there, and in spite of good intentions and serious efforts, the stress model just will not always work. This is the time the teacher must turn to other resources, both within the school system and outside of it. It is crucial to recognize that all helping professionals need advice from time to time and it is certainly not an unprofessional act to seek assistance, nor is it a sign of incompetence.

General Considerations for Teacher Intervention

There are a number of suggestions for making the model work for those who want to be helpful to children under stress. One practice that teachers have found useful is to limit the number of interventions employed with a child at one time. Too many interventions may have a negative interactive effect and in turn may act as stressors. Also, it is important to know which strategies seem to work, with which children. Limiting the number of interventions allows this assessment to be made.

Once a strategy has been selected and implemented, the model calls for a monitoring process to determine its effects, if any. The best advice at this point is to give the intervention strategy a chance to work. Some of the most powerful strategies, such as attempts to shift the child's perception of locus of control, require a considerable period of time. In these instances the teacher should be looking for signs of progress rather than the unlikely overnight transformation. Even the butterfly takes time to change from a caterpillar. Unfortunately, the model can offer no specific time periods to be relied upon. The decision about whether to continue a strategy or shift to another is largely a personal judgment based upon the severity of the stressors, the general response patterns of the child, the specific response of the child to the stressor, the teachers's comfort level with the child and the child's responses, and the teacher's best estimate of the effects of the intervention and its promise if continued.

Earlier in the chapter it was noted that, for the child with multiple stressors, it is appropriate and often useful to select one stressor upon which to focus the intervention. The stressor selected may not be the one considered to be the most severe for the child, but it might be a stressor that may be the most likely to yield to intervention. The reduction in the overall stress in the child by successfully addressing one stressor or response may greatly reduce the cumulative effect of multiple stressors.

Keep in mind that sometimes a reactive intervention strategy can have a proactive effect. This may happen on the individual level, the group level, or possibly both. If a teacher reads a story about the death of a pet (such as *The Tenth Good Thing About Barney*; Viorst, 1971), with a child whose pet had died, this may not only help the child process the death of the pet but also provide the child with a better understanding of death generally, which may be drawn upon later in the event of the death of a relative. Second, if the same story is read with a small group or an entire class, primarily to assist one child in the group, a long-range proactive effect might occur for other children in the group who later encounter death as a stressor.

One other point needs to be repeated. In the professional role, a teacher has sustained contacts with a group of children for approximately five hours per day for 165 to 180 days per year. No adult outside of the home has this kind of sustained contact and opportunity for influence. No other helping professional even comes close to this amount of sustained contact. The teacher should not diminish the potential for influence that exists. While the teacher's role certainly involves the development of the cognitive processes of the child, and while that role must be attended to, there does seem to be time and there is an obvious need for the teacher to attend to the psychosocial needs of the child as well. This is especially true since the cognitive development and the psychosocial development of the child are so intertwined. Teachers should remember that they do not have to be therapists to be therapeutic.

REFERENCES
NAME INDEX
SUBJECT INDEX

References

Adams, J. D. (1978). Improving stress management. *Social Change, Ideas and Applications, 8,* (4), 1–3, 9–12.

American Education Reprint. (1976). *Education of the handicapped today and a bill of rights for the handicapped.* Washington, DC: U.S. Government Printing Office.

Anthony, E.J. (1974). The syndrome of the psychologically invulnerable child. In E. J. Anthony & C. Koupernick (Eds.), *The child and his family: Children at psychiatric risk* (pp. 529–544). New York: John Wiley.

Anthony, E. J. (1975). Naturalistic studies of disturbed families. In E. J. Anthony (Ed.), *Explorations in child psychiatry (pp. 344–378). New York: Plenum Press.*

Anthony, S. (1971). *The discovery of death in childhood and after.* London: Penguin Press.

Armor, D. J., Polich, M. J., & Braiker, H. B. (1980). Rand reports. *Psychiatric News, 15,* 8.

Bane, M. J. (1976). Marital disruption and the lives of children. *Journal of Social Issues 32* (1), 109–110.

Bemporad, J., & Wuhl, C. (1978). Psychosomatic disorders. In E. Gilbert (Ed.), *Psychosocial aspects of pediatric care* (pp. 155–169). New York: Grune and Stratton.

Bleuler, M. (1974). The offspring of schizophrenics. *Schizophrenia Bulletin, 8,* 93–107.

Blom, G. E. (1958). The reactions of hospitalized children to illness. *Pediatrics, 22,* 590–600.

Blom, G. E. (1971). *The role of emotions in childhood asthma.* Unpublished manuscript.

Blom, G. E. (1978). The role of content in the teaching of reading. In J. Samuels (Ed.), *What research has to say about reading instruction* (pp. 86–94). Newark, DE: International Reading Association.

Blom, G. E. (1979, November). *Children's books and reading.* Paper presented at the Fifteenth Annual Preschool and Early Childhood Conference, Rochester, MI.

Blom, G. E. (1980a). *Emotional aftermath of a disaster: The 1980 Kalamazoo tornado.* Unpublished manuscript, Michigan State University, East Lansing.

Blom, G. E. (1980b). [School district mobility data related to family forms]. Unpublished raw data.

Blom, G. E. (1981). Psychological reactions of a school population to a skywalk accident. In C.D. Speilberger, I. G. Sarason, & N. A. Milgram (Eds.), *Stress and anxiety* (Vol. 8, pp. 361–370). Washington, DC: Hemisphere Publishing.

Blom, G. E. (1984). Children who cope. In R. P. Boger, G. E. Blom, & L. E. Lezotte (Eds.), *Child nurturance: Vol. 4. Child nurturing in the 1980's* (pp. 65–87). New York: Plenum Press.

Blom, G. E., Cheney, B. D., & Snoddy, J. E. (1982). *MSU program cork drinking/non-drinking curriculum for teachers.* East Lansing, MI: Michigan State University.

Brooks, A. (1982, March 7). Helping youngsters face a move. *The New York Times,* p. D2.

Camp, B. W., & Bash, M. A. (1981). *Think aloud: Increasing social and cognitive skills—A problem solving program for children.* Champaign, IL: Research Press.

Camp, B. W., Blom, G. E., Hebert, F., & van Doorninck, W. J. (1977). Think aloud, a program for developing self-control in young aggressive boys. *Journal of Abnormal Clinical Psychology, 5,* 157–169.

Cannon, W. B. (1929). *Bodily changes in pain, hunger, fear and rage.* New York: Appleton Press.

Carro, G. (1980, June). What worries kids most? *Ladies Home Journal,* p. 126.

Center for Law and Education. (1978). Corporal punishment in the schools. *Inequality in Education, 23.*

Childers, P., & Wimmer, M. (1971). *The concept of death in early childhood. Child Development, 42,* 1299.

Children's Defense Fund. (1979). *America's children and their families: Key facts.* Washington, DC: Author.

Cianciolo, P. (1975). Feeling books develop social and personal sensitivities. *Elementary English, 52,* 37–42.

Clark, J., Liberman-Lascoe, R., & Hyman, J. A. (1980, April). *An analysis of corporal punishment cases as reported in nationwide newspapers: Types, incidents and outcomes.* Paper presented at the annual meeting of the National Association of School Psychologists, Washington, DC.

Coddington, R. D. (1972). The significance of life events as etiologic factors in the diseases of children. *Journal of Psychosomatic Research, 16,* 7–18.

Coles, R. (1964). *Children of crisis.* Boston: Little Brown.

Collins, G. (1981, February 2). The stigma of one-parent homes. *New York Times,* p. A16.

Cooke, R., & Parsons, P. (1963). The listening class: An opportunity to advance skills of attending to, concentrating on and utilizing auditory information in emotionally disturbed children. *The Journal of Special Education, 2,* 329–336.

Coopersmith, S. (1975). *Developing motivation in young children.* San Francisco: Albion Press.

Cottle, T. J. (1980). *Children's secrets.* Garden City, NY: Anchor Press.

Dallas, D. (1978). Savagery, show and tell. *American Psychologist, 33,* 388–390.

Diamond, J. E. (1982, September 14). Children under stress: The causes and cures. *Family Weekly,* pp. 4–6.

Divorce American style. (1983, January 10). *Newsweek,* p. 42.

Dreikurs, R., & Grey, L. (1968). *A new approach to discipline: Logical consequences.* New York: Hawthorn Press.

Dreyer, S. S. (1977). *The book finder: A guide to children's literature about the needs and problems of youth aged 2–15.* Circle Pines, MN: American Guidance Services.

Elkind, D. (1974). *Children and adolescents: Interpretative essays on Jean Piaget.* New York: Oxford University Press.

Elkind, D. (1982). *The hurried child: Growing up too fast too soon.* Reading, MA: Addison-Wesley.

Erickson, E. L., McEvoy, A. W., & Colucci, N. D. (1979). *Child abuse and neglect: A guidebook for educators and community leaders.* Holmes Beach, FL: Learning Publications.

Fassler, J. (1978). *Helping children cope.* New York: Free Press.

Finn, P., & O'Gorman, P. A. (1981). *Teaching about alcohol: Concepts, methods, and classroom activities.* Boston: Allyn and Bacon.

Freese, A. S. (1979). *Understanding stress* (Public Affairs Pamphlet No. 538). (Available from author, 381 Park Avenue South, New York 10016.)

Gage, N., & Berliner, D. (1979). *Educational psychology.* Chicago: Rand McNally.

Gallup, G. H. (1978). The tenth annual Gallup poll of the public attitudes toward the public schools. *Phi Delta Kappan, 9,* 33–45.

Gardner, R. (1971). *Boys and girls book about divorce.* New York: Science House.

Gardner, R. (1973). *The family book about minimal brain dysfunction.* New York: Jason Aronson.

Garmezy, N. (1970). Vulnerable children: Implications derived from studies of an internalizing-externalizing symptom dimension. In J. Zubin & A. M. Freedman (Eds.), *The psychopathology of adolescence* (pp. 212–239). New York: Grune and Stratton.

Garmezy, N. (1974). The study of competence in children at risk for severe psychopathology. In E. J. Anthony & C. Koupernik (Eds.), *The child in his family: Children at psychiatric risk* (pp. 77–98). New York: John Wiley.

Garmezy, N. (1981). Children under stress: Perspectives on antecedents and correlates of vulnerability and resistance to psychopathology. In A. I. Rabin, J. Aranoff, A. M. Barclay, & R. A. Zucker (Eds.), *Further explorations in personality* (pp. 196–269). New York: John Wiley.

Germeroth, S. R. (1978). *Why teach stress management and stress control?* ERIC Document Reproduction Service No. ED 150 145.

Ginnott, H. (1972). *Teacher and child.* New York: Macmillan.

Glasser, W. (1969). *Schools without failure.* New York: Harper & Row.

Gordon, T. (1974). *Teacher effectiveness training.* New York: Wyden.

Gould, M. S., Wunsch-Hitzig, R., & Dohrenwend, B. (1981). Estimating the prevalence of childhood psychopathology. *Journal of the American Academy of Child Psychiatry, 20,* 462–476.

Governor's Task Force on School Violence and Vandalism. (1978). *Report and recommendations.* Lansing, MI: State of Michigan.

Group for the Advancement of Psychiatry. (1973). *The joys and sorrows of parenthood.* New York: Scribner's.

Haan, N. (1977). *Coping and defending: Processes of self-environment organization*. New York: Academic Press.

Harris, J. D. (1959). *Normal children and mothers*. Glencoe, IL: Glencoe Free Press.

Helfer, R. E., & Kempe, C. H. (Eds). (1968). *The battered child*. Chicago: University of Chicago Press.

Helfer, R. E., & Kempe, C. H. (Eds.). (1976). *Child abuse and neglect: The family and the community*. Cambridge, MA: Ballinger.

Hentoff, N. (1980, April). Child abuse in the schools. *Ladies Home Journal*, p. 101.

Holmes, T. H., & Rahe, R. H. (1967). The social readjustment rating scale. *Journal of Psychosomatic Research, 11*, 213.

Howland, R. W., & Howland, J. W. (1978). 200 years of drinking in the United States: Evolution of the disease concept. In J. A. Ewing & B. A. Rouse (Eds.), *Drinking: Alcohol in American society: Issues and current research* (pp. 39–60). Chicago: Nelson-Hall.

Hyman, J. A., & Wise, J. H. (Eds.). (1979). *Corporal punishment in American education*. Philadelphia: Temple University Press.

Ingall, C. (1983). *Use of children's literature in elementary school children's stress*. Unpublished manuscript.

International Youth Library. (1982). *Bibliography of books for handicapped children* (Studies on Books and Reading, No. 11). Paris: UNESCO.

Jahoda, G., & Cramond, J. (1972). *Children and alcohol*. London: Her Majesty's Stationery Office.

Kealey, R. (1981, December). Student mobility and its effects on achievement. *Phi Delta Kappan, 66*, 276–277.

Kempe, C. H. (1962). The battered child syndrome. *Journal of the American Medical Association, 181*, 17–24.

Kempe, C. H., Silver, H. K., & O'Brien, D. (1976). *Current pediatric diagnosis treatment* (4th ed.). Los Altos, CA: Lange Medical Publications.

Kempe, C. H., & Helfer, R. E. (Eds.). (1980). *The battered child*. Chicago: University of Chicago Press.

Kendall, P. C., & Hollan, S. D. (Eds.). (1979). *Cognitive-behavioral interventions: Theory, research, and procedures*. New York: Academic Press.

Keniston, K. (1977). *All our children: The American family under pressure*. New York: Harcourt Brace Jovanovich.

Kesselman-Turkel, J., & Peterson, F. (1981). *Test taking strategies*. Chicago: Contemporary Press.

Kids need caring adults. (1984, February 8). *Lansing State Journal*, p. 13.

Kliman, A. S. (1978). *Crisis: psychological first aid for recovery and growth*. New York: Holt, Rinehart and Winston.

Kliman, G. (1968). *Psychological emergencies of childhood*. New York: Grune and Stratton.

Kounin, J. (1970). *Discipline and group management in classrooms*. New York: Holt, Rinehart & Winston.

Large, R. (1978). Flipping the coin: From test anxiety to test wiseness. *Journal of Reading, 22*, 274–277.

Lazarus, R. S. (1966). *Psychological stress and the coping process*. New York: McGraw-Hill.

Lazarus, R. S. (1977). Cognitive and coping process in emotion. In A. Monat & R. S. Lazarus (Eds.), *Stress and coping: An anthology* (pp. 145–158). New York: Columbia University Press.

Lefcourt, H. M. (1976). *Locus of control: Current trends in theory and research.* Hillsdale, NJ: Lawrence Erlbaum Associates.

McDonnell, E., & Friedman, R. H. (1978, March). *An analysis of editorial opinion regarding corporal punishment: Some dynamics of regional differences.* Paper presented at the National Association of School Psychologists, New York City.

McGuffey's Fourth Eclectic Reader. (1879). Cincinnati: Eclectic Press.

Meichenbaum, D. (1976). A self-instructional approach to stress management: A proposal for stress inoculation training. In C. Speilberger & I. Sarason (Eds.), *Stress and anxiety* (Vol. 1, pp. 237–263). Washington, DC: Hemisphere Publishing.

Michigan, State of. (1974) *Children's Protective Services in Michigan* (DSS Publication 105). Lansing, MI: Department of Social Services.

Money, J. (1977). The syndrome of abuse dwarfism (Psychosocial dwarfism or reversible hyposomatotrophism). *American Journal of Diseases of Childhood, 131,* 508–512.

Moos, R., & Billings, A. (1982). Conceptualizing and measuring coping resources and processes. In L. Goldberger & S. Brenitz (Eds.), *Handbook of stress: Theoretical and clinical aspects* (pp. 212–230). New York: Free Press.

Morris, K. (1982). *Anthony: A case study.* Unpublished manuscript, Michigan State University, East Lansing, MI.

Morse, W., & Ravlin, M. (1979). Psychoeducation in the school setting. In S. I. Harrison (Ed.), *Basic handbook of child psychiatry: Vol. 3. Therapeutic Interventions* (pp. 333–352). New York: Basic Books.

Murphy, L. B. (1981). Explorations in child personality. In A. I. Rabin, J. Aronoff, A. M. Barclay, & R. A. Zucker (Eds.), *Further explorations in personality* (pp. 161–195). New York: John Wiley.

Murphy, L. B., & Moriarity, A. E. (1976). *Vulnerability, coping and growth from infancy to adolescence.* New Haven: Yale University Press.

National Committee for Prevention of Child Abuse. (1982). *A message from Rod McKuen: An appeal for funds.* Chicago, IL: Author.

National Institute of Education. (1978). *Violent schools, safe schools: A safe school study report to Congress.* Washington, DC: U.S. Government Printing Office.

Neuchterlein, K. H. (1970). *Competent disadvantaged children: A research.* Unpublished summa cum laude doctoral dissertation, University of Minnesota, Minneapolis.

Nirje, B. (1969). The normalization principle and its human management implications. In R. Keegel & A. Shearer (Eds.), *Changing patterns in residential services for the mentally retarded* (pp. 179–195). Washington, DC: President's Committee on Mental Retardation.

Ogg, E. (1976). *One-parent families* (Public Affairs Pamphlet No. 543). New York: Public Affairs Committee.

Olweus, D. (1978). *Aggression in the schools: Bullies and whipping boys.* New York: Halstead Press.

Palomares, U. H., & Rubini, T. (1974). *Magic circle.* La Mesa, CA: Human Development Training Institute.

Perry, H., & Perry, S. E. (1959). *The schoolhouse disasters: Family and community as determinants of the child's response to disaster. Disaster study number II.* Washington, DC: National Academy of Sciences National Research Council.

Phillips, B. (1978). *School stress and anxiety: Theory research and intervention.* New York: Human Sciences Press.

President's Commission on Mental Health. (1978). *Report to the President* (Report No. 040–000–00390–8). Washington, DC: U.S. Government Printing Office.

Ramos, S. (1975). *Teaching your child to cope with crisis.* New York: McKay.

Redl, F. (1959). Strategies and techniques in the life space interview. *American Journal of Orthopsychiatry, 29,* 1–18.

Riggs, C. W. (1978). *Bibliotherapy: An annotated bibliography.* Newark, DE: International Reading Association.

Rosenblatt, R. (1983). *Children of war.* New York: Anchor Press, Doubleday.

Ross, H. (1965). The teacher game. *The Psychoanalytic Study of the Child, 20,* 288–297.

Rossman, H. M., & Kohrweiler, J. B. (1977). Relaxation training with intermediate grade students. *Elementary School Guidance Counseling, 2,* 259–266.

Rutter, M. (1979). Proactive factors in children's responses to stress and disadvantage. In M. W. Kent & J. E. Rolf (Eds.), *Primary prevention of psychopathology: Vol. 3. Social competence in children* (pp. 49–74). Hanover, NH: University Press of New England.

Rutter, M. (1983). Stress, coping and development: Some issues and some questions. In N. Garmezy & M. Rutter (Eds.), *Stress, coping and development in children* (pp. 1–41). New York: McGraw-Hill.

Rutter, M., Maughan, B., Mortimore, P., Ouston, J., & Smith, A. (1979). *Fifteen thousand hours: Secondary schools and their effects on children.* Cambridge, MA: Harvard University Press.

Sanoff, A. (1982). Our neglected children. *U.S. News and World Report, 93*(6), 54–58.

Satchell, M. (1985, March 24). Should children be hit in school? *The New York Times,* pp. A 4–5.

Schneider, M., & Robin, A. (1973). *The turtle manual.* Stony Brook, NY: Point of Woods Laboratory School, State University of New York.

Schneider, M., & Robin, A. (1976). The turtle technique: A method for the self-control of impulsive behavior. In J. D. Krumbotz & C. E. Thoreson (Eds.), *Counseling methods* (pp. 141–156). New York: Holt, Rinehart and Winston.

Schultz, E. W. (1980). Teaching coping skills for stress and anxiety. *Teaching Exceptional Children, 13,* 12–15.

Schwartz, S. (1977). Death education: Suggested readings and audiovisuals. *Journal of School Health, 12,* 607–609.

Segal, J., & Yahraes, H. (1978). *A child's journey: Forces that shape the lives of our young.* New York: McGraw-Hill.

Selye, H. (1956). *The stress of life.* New York: McGraw-Hill.

Shore, M. F. (Ed.). (1967). *Red is the color of hurting: Planning for children in the hospital.* Bethesda, MD: National Institute of Mental Health.

Slavin, R. E. (1980). *Non-cooperative outcomes of cooperative learning*. Baltimore, MD: Johns Hopkins University, Center for Social Organization of Schools.

Spivack, G., Platt, J., & Shure, M. (1976). *The problem-solving approach to adjustment*. Washington, DC: Jossey-Bass.

Springer, K. (1983, December 21). Why Johnny can't cope. *Lansing State Journal*, pp. 2–3.

Starr, R. H. (1979). Child abuse. *American Psychologist 34*(10), 872–878.

Stevenson, R. L. (1915). *Treasure island*. New York: Rand McNally.

Tringo, J. L. (1970). The hierarchy of preference toward disability groups. *The Journal of Special Education, 4*, 295–306.

U.S. Department of Health, Education and Welfare. (1974). *Books that help children deal with a hospital experience* (DHEW Publication No. HSA 78–5224). Washington, DC: U.S. Government Printing Office.

Viorst, J. (1971). *The tenth good thing about Barney*. New York: Atheneum Press.

Wallerstein, J. S., & Kelley, J. B. (1980a). California's children of divorce. *Psychology Today, 13*, 67–68.

Wallerstein, J. S., & Kelly, J. B. (1980b). *Surviving the breakup: How children and parents cope with divorce*. New York: Basic Books.

Weintraub, S. A. (1973). Self-control as a correlate of an internalizing-externalizing symptom dimension. *Journal of Abnormal Child Psychology, 1*, 292–307.

Werner, E. E., & Smith, R. S. (1982). *Vulnerable but invincible: A study of resilient children*. New York: McGraw-Hill.

White, R. W. (1979). Competence as an aspect of personal growth. In M. W. Kent & J. E. Rolf (Eds.), *Social competence in children* (pp. 5–22). Hanover, NH: University Press of New England.

Whitt, J. K. (1984). Children's adaptation to chronic illness and handicapping conditions. In M. G. Eisenberg, L. C. Sutkin, & M. A. Jansen (Eds.), *Chronic illness and disability through the life span* (pp. 69–102). New York: Springer.

Wolfensberger, W. (1972). *The principle of normalization in human services*. Toronto: National Institute of Mental Retardation.

Wolfenstein, M. (1977). *Disaster: A psychological essay*. New York: Arno Press.

Wolff, S. (1981). *Children under stress*. London: Penguin Books.

Yamamoto, K. (1979). Children's ratings of the stressfulness of experiences. *Developmental Psychology, 15*, 581–582.

Zimet, S. (Ed.). (1975). *What children read in school*. New York: Grune and Stratton.

Zucker, M. E., & Snoddy, J. E. (1980). What teachers think they can do about stress conditions in childhood. *Cork Communicator, 2*, 1–2.

Name Index

197

Subject Index

Italicized numbers refer to pages on which tables or figures are located.